ZOOM IN ...

Nine Eleven

Herausgegeben und erarbeitet von:
Iris Faßbender und Colette Granvillano

Schöningh

Muttersprachliche Betreuung: Elin Arbin

www.schoeningh-schulbuch.de
Schöningh Verlag, Jühenplatz 1–3, 33098 Paderborn

Druck 5 4 3 2 1 / Jahr 2017 16 15 14 13
Die letzte Zahl bezeichnet das Jahr dieses Druckes.

Umschlaggestaltung: Reinhild Kassing, Kassel
Umschlagabbildung: picture-alliance/dpa
Druck und Bindung: westermann druck GmbH, Braunschweig

ISBN 978-3-14-040650-5

Zur Arbeit mit dem Buch

Anforderungsbereiche

Alle Aufgaben dieses Bandes sind farbig gekennzeichnet und sind somit den drei Anforderungsbereichen eindeutig zuzuordnen. Eine detaillierte Aufstellung aller Operatoren finden Sie im Anhang.

AFB I: Comprehension

AFB II: Analysis

AFB III: Evaluation/Re-creation of text

Aufgaben, die einen Text inhaltlich/sprachlich vorbereiten beziehungsweise weiterführend vertiefen, sind grau unterlegt.

Symbole

Auf verschiedenen Seiten dieses Bandes finden Sie Symbole, die auf sprachlich-methodische Fertigkeiten, Musterlösungen und weiterführende Aktivitäten hinweisen.

Speaking – Mithilfe dieser Aufgabe wird der mündliche Ausdruck geübt.

Listening – Zu diesem Material gibt es im Lehrerband eine Audio-Datei (auf CD), mit der das Hörverstehen geschult wird.

Mediation – Dieses Material wird in eigenen Worten auf Englisch wiedergegeben und dient der Sprachmittlung.

Model solution – Zu dieser Aufgabe liegt eine Musterlösung vor.

Activity – Bei dieser Aufgabe werden die Schülerinnen und Schüler in vielfältiger Weise selbst aktiv.

Netcodes

Netcodes verweisen auf Zusatzmaterial im Internet und erleichtern Ihnen das Auffinden von Links und Dateien, die speziell für den vorliegenden Band ausgewählt oder erstellt wurden.

Netcode 40650-000

Zur Nutzung gehen Sie bitte auf folgende Seite: http://www.schoeningh-schulbuch.de/netcode

Dort geben Sie dann den 8-stelligen Code ein und gelangen so zu dem jeweiligen Material.

Contents

Getting started

7:59 A.M.	8:14 A.M.	8:20 A.M.	8:42 A.M.	8:45 A.M.	9:03 A.M.	9:40 A.M.
American Airlines Flight 11 with 92 people on board departs from Boston to L.A.	United Airlines Flight 175 with 65 people on board departs from Boston to L.A.	American Airlines Flight 77 with 64 people on board departs from Washington to L.A.	United Airlines Flight 93 with 44 people on board departs from Newark to San Francisco.	American Airlines Flight 11 crashes into the north tower.	United Airlines Flight 175 crashes into the south tower.	American Airlines Flight 77 crashes into the west side of the Pentagon.

A child's drawing of 9/11

"I was born in 1965 in Los Angeles. I am 37 years old. I became an American on September 11, 2001."
Karen Kehela, co-chairman of Imagine Films and executive producer of the film *A Beautiful Mind*, in *O – The Oprah Magazine*

With reference to the two pictures provided here, explain this quotation against the backdrop of your previous knowledge about the 9/11 attacks and their impact on the American psyche.

9:45 A.M.	9:59 A.M.	10:07 A.M.	10:10 A.M.	10:28 A.M.	5:30 P.M.	8:30 P.M.
A passenger on Flight 93 calls an operator and reports that the plane has been hijacked.	The south tower collapses.	United Airlines Flight 93 crashes near Shanksville, Pennsylvania.	A section of the Pentagon collapses.	The north tower collapses.	World Trade Center 7 collapses.	President George W. Bush addresses the nation from the Oval Office.

Preliminary Events: Paving the Way to 9/11?

M1 Criminals or Crusaders?

The US-Austrian psychiatrist and aggression researcher Frederick J. Hacker (1914–1989) specialized in the field of terrorism research. In 1976, he published a categorization of terrorists in his work *Crusaders, Criminals and Crazies: Terror and Terrorism in Our Time*. Though these categories have undergone some minor changes, they are still considered valid today.

1. As described in the introduction to the text, Hacker distinguished between "crazies", "criminals" and "crusaders". What do you associate with the term "crusader"? Make use of the illustration and make an educated guess on the differences between a "crazy", a "criminal" and a "crusader".

2. **Present** the three different categories of terrorists as put forward by Hacker and **state** why this distinction can be helpful for law enforcement agencies.

crusader *Kreuzfahrer*

to transgress to do sth. that is not allowed by a law, custom, or religion

[...] Frederick Hacker suggests three categories of persons who commit terrorism: *crazies, criminals and crusaders**. He notes that an individual carrying out a terrorist act is seldom "purely" one type or the other, but suggests that each type offers some insights into why an individual will resort to terrorism. [...]

Hacker offers some ideas on what is subsumed under each label. **Crazies**, he suggests, are *emotionally disturbed individuals who are driven to commit terrorism "by reasons of their own that often do not make sense to anybody else."*

Criminals, on the other hand, *perform terrorist acts for more easily understood reasons: personal gain*. Such individuals transgress* the laws of society knowingly and, one assumes, in full possession of their faculties*. Both their motives and their goals are usually clear, if deplorable*, to most of mankind.

This is not the case with the **crusaders**. These individuals commit terrorism for reasons that are often unclear to themselves and to those witnessing the acts. Their ultimate goals are frequently even less understandable. While such individuals are usually idealistically inspired, their idealism tends to be a mixed bag of half-understood philosophies.

Crusaders, according to Hacker, *seek not personal gain, but prestige and power for a collective cause*. They commit terrorist acts in the belief "that they are serving a higher cause," in Hacker's assessment.

faculty any of the physical or mental abilities that a person is born with
deplorable making you feel shocked

What difference does it make what kind of terrorist is behind the machine gun or bomb? To the law enforcement personnel charged with resolving the hostage* situation, it can be crucial to know what type of person is controlling the situation. Criminals can be offered sufficient personal gains or security provisions to induce* them to release the hostages. Crusaders are far less likely to be talked out of carrying out their threats by inducements of personal gains, since to do so they would have to betray, in some sense, that higher cause for which they are committing the action. [...]

hostage a person who is the prisoner of sb. who threatens to kill them if they do not get what they want
to induce sb. to do sth. to persuade sb. to do sth.

[I]t is true that the majority of individuals who commit modern terrorism are, or perceive themselves to be, crusaders. According to Hacker, the typical crusading terrorist appears to be normal, no matter how crazy the cause or how criminal the means for this cause may seem. He or she is neither an idiot nor a fool. Instead, the crusading terrorist is frequently a professional, well trained, well prepared, and well disciplined in the habit of blind obedience* to a cause.

obedience doing what sb. tells you to do

HACKER'S TYPOLOGY OF TERRORISTS

Type of Terrorist	Motive/Goal	Willing to Negotiate?	Expectation of Survival
Criminal	Personal gain/profit	Usually, in return for profit and/or safe passage	Strong
Crusader	"Higher cause" (usually a blend of religious and political cause)	Seldom, since to do so could be seen as a betrayal of the cause	Minimal, since death offers reward in "afterlife"
Crazy	Clear only to perpetrator	Possible, but only if negotiator can understand motive	Strong, but not based on reality

Cynthia C. Combs, "Terrorism in the 21st Century", Pearson, London 2012

M2 "Ich durchlief eine Gehirnwäsche" – Interview mit Tawfik Hamid

Jonathan Stock

Tawfik Hamid used to be a member of a radical terror organization. Today, the scientist fights against extremism with the help of the Koran. The online version of the German newspaper *Die Zeit* conducted an interview with him in which he explains how and why he developed a jihadist's mindset.

1. **Point out** the different steps Hamid underwent in the process of turning into a jihadist.

2. **State** the other reasons put forward by Hamid that make people turn towards fundamentalism.

3. Against the backdrop of Hacker's categorization (cf. **M1**), **assess** what type of potential terrorist Hamid would have been. Give reasons for your answer.

Tawfik Hamid

ZEIT ONLINE Muss ich Angst vor Ihnen haben, Dr. Hamid?
HAMID Nein, ich habe den Pfad der Gewalt* mittlerweile verlassen. Aber vor 25 Jahren hätten Sie Angst haben müssen. [...] Ich hätte Sie gehasst. Damals war ich Mitglied der Terrororganisation Islamischer Dschihad. Ich war radikal, jung und kurz davor, im Namen Allahs zu töten. [...] Ich durchlief eine regelrechte Gehirnwäsche*.
ZEIT ONLINE Wie kann man sich das vorstellen?
HAMID Als einen mehrstufigen*, multidimensionalen Prozess. Stufe eins: Alle kritischen Gedanken unterdrücken. Bevor ich die Moschee [in Kairo] betrat, sagte man mir: „Dein Gehirn ist wie ein Affe. Der kann dich zwar zum Palast des Königs bringen, aber sobald du drin bist, solltest du ihn draußen lassen." Also: Glauben, nicht denken. Das erste Gebet war wie die Aufstellung* vor einer Schlacht: Schulter an Schulter und Fuß an Fuß. Ich fühlte mich sofort als Teil von etwas Größerem, Heiligem.
Später nahmen sie mich beiseite, boten mir eine Führungsposition* an – ich fühlte mich geschmeichelt*. In den Monaten, die folgten, erklärte man mir, was richtig und was falsch ist. Das gab ein süßes, fast friedliches Gefühl von Macht. Auch ich konnte jetzt anderen Leuten sagen, was richtig und falsch ist, alles war klar und geordnet, ich musste mir keine Sorgen machen, solange ich allen Befehlen folgte*. [...]
ZEIT ONLINE Wurden Sie aufgefordert, Terrorakte zu begehen?
HAMID Ja. Anfang der achtziger Jahre war ich bereit, nach Afghanistan zu gehen und gegen die Russen in den Krieg zu ziehen. Es wäre sehr einfach gewesen: Nur meinen Namen hätte ich registrieren lassen müssen – um Flug, Geld und Visa hätte sich die Organisation gekümmert. Dann machte man mir in einer kleinen Gruppe das Angebot, einen Polizisten umzubringen, sein Grab zu schaufeln* und ihn lebendig zu begraben*. Das war der Moment, wo mein Gewissen* und meine Erziehung zurückkehrten. Ich begann aufzuwachen – und lehnte ab.
ZEIT ONLINE Sie kehrten dem Islamischen Dschihad den Rücken*, verließen Ägypten und sind heute einer der schärfsten Kritiker des radikalen Islam. Was bringt Menschen immer wieder dazu, gewaltbereit zu werden?
HAMID Jeder hat seine Gründe. Bei mir spielte die Liebe zur arabischen Sprache eine große Rolle. Von einem Imam in der wundervollen Sprache des Koran unterrichtet zu werden ist eine mächtige, überwältigende* Erfahrung, die nur schwer zu vermitteln ist – man hört das klare, direkte Wort Allahs!
So ähnlich muss sich Moses gefühlt haben, als Gott ihm die zehn Gebote* diktierte. Dieses Werkzeug* kann zum Guten und Bösen eingesetzt werden – bei mir war es eben zum Bösen.
Andere haben Angst vor dem Höllenfeuer* oder glauben einfach, das Richtige zu tun. Arme freuen sich über das Geld, mit dem sie heiraten können, sexuell Frustrierte auf die Jungfrauen, die sie erwarten. Im radikalen Islam ist es verboten, Frauen zu berühren oder auch nur anzugucken. Daneben werden aber die erotischen Passagen der Schriften

Pfad der Gewalt path of violence
eine Gehirnwäsche durchlaufen to be brainwashed
mehrstufig multi-levelled
Aufstellung deployment
Führungsposition leading position
geschmeichelt flattered
Befehlen folgen to obey orders
ein Grab schaufeln to dig a grave
jdn. lebendig begraben to bury sb. alive
Gewissen conscience
etw. den Rücken kehren to turn one's back on sth.
überwältigend overwhelming
die zehn Gebote the Ten Commandments
Werkzeug tool
Höllenfeuer hellfire

regelmäßig zitiert, recht deutliche Beschreibungen der Frauen, die im Paradies auf einen warten! Irgendwann denkt man, dass Sex für einen eben nur dort möglich ist – und dann versucht man, so schnell wie möglich dorthin zu kommen.

ZEIT ONLINE [...] Sie müssen von vielen Hardlinern als Verräter* angesehen werden. Wie ist es um Ihre Sicherheit bestellt?

HAMID Mein Haus ist gesichert, ich ziehe oft um, werde bei Veranstaltungen von Sicherheitskräften begleitet. Ich lebe so seit 20 Jahren, ich habe mich daran gewöhnt.

ZEIT ONLINE Haben Sie keine Angst?

HAMID Nein.

ZEIT ONLINE Warum nicht?

HAMID Ich vertraue auf Allah.

Jonathan Stock, „Ich durchlief eine Gehirnwäsche“, www.zeit.de, 03.12.2009 [04.09.2012]

Verräter traitor

4. Some people claim that 9/11 was more or less a “self-made catastrophe”, pointing out a connection between the US’s – especially the CIA’s – involvement in Afghanistan in the 1980s and the 9/11 attacks. Do further research on the war in Afghanistan that Hamid refers to in this interview in order to explain how one might come to this conclusion. In class, discuss the feasibility of this connection.

M3 The Reluctant Fundamentalist

Mohsin Hamid

The novel *The Reluctant Fundamentalist* is set in a café in Lahore, Pakistan, where a Pakistani man named Changez tells his story to an apparently nervous American listener. In the course of the novel, the reader reader learns about Changez’ relationship with an American woman and about the factors which slowly but surely contributed to his abandonment of America.

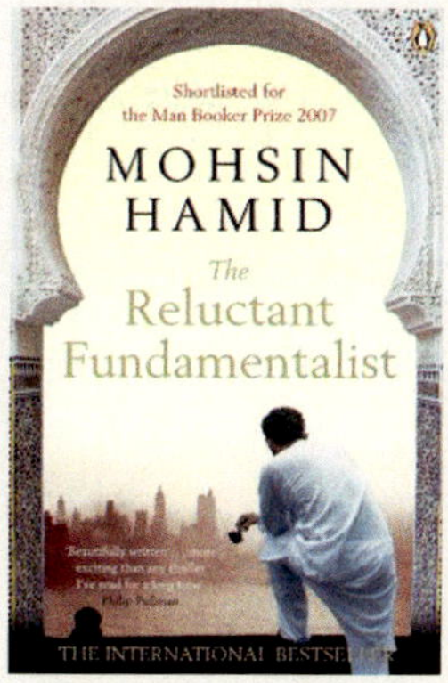

1. Look up definitions of “fundamentalism” and “oxymoron”. Then discuss in class in how far the title of this novel can be considered an oxymoron.

2. **Describe** the relationship between Changez and the US as presented in these extracts.

3. **Examine** the narrative techniques employed by the author in order to give Changez’ account an air of reliability and credibility.

4. Put yourself into the shoes of the American listener and write his interior monologue while listening to Changez. What is your impression of Changez? How do you feel about his utterances concerning the US?

Extract from chapter 1

Excuse me, sir, but may I be of assistance? Ah, I see I have alarmed you. Do not be frightened by my beard: I am a lover of America. I noticed that you were looking for something; more than looking, in fact you seemed to be on a *mission*, and since I am both a native of this city and a speaker of your language, I thought I might offer you my services.

How did I know you were American? No, not by the color of your skin; we have a range of complexions* in this country, and yours occurs often among the people of our northwest frontier. Nor was it your dress that gave you away; a European tourist could easily have purchased in Des Moines your suit, with its single vent*, and your button-down shirt. True, your hair, short-cropped, and your expansive chest – the chest, I would say, of a man who bench-presses regularly, and maxes out* well above two-twenty-five – are typical of a certain *type* of American; but then again, sportsmen and soldiers of all nationalities tend to look alike. Instead, it was your *bearing* that allowed me to identify you, and I do not mean that as an insult, for I see your face has hardened, but merely as an observation.

complexion the appearance of the skin on sb.'s face (e.g. dark, fair)
vent a straight cut at the bottom of a piece of clothes
to max out (AmE inf.) to reach the limit of sth.

Extract from chapter 5

The following evening was supposed to be our last in Manila. I was in my room, packing my things. I turned on the television and saw what at first I took to be a film. But as I continued to watch, I realized that it was not fiction but news. I stared as one – and then the other – of the twin towers of New York's World Trade Center collapsed. And then I *smiled*. Yes, despicable* as it may sound, my initial reaction was to be remarkably pleased. Your disgust is evident; indeed, your large hand has, perhaps without noticing, clenched into a fist. But please believe me when I tell you that I am no sociopath [...]. But at that moment, my thoughts were not with the *victims* of the attack – death on television moves me most when it is fictitious and happens to characters with whom I have built up relationships over multiple episodes – no, I was caught up in the *symbolism* of it all, the fact that someone had so visibly brought America to her knees. Ah, I see I am only compounding* your displeasure. I understand, of course; it is hateful to hear another person gloat over* one's country's misfortune. But surely you cannot be completely innocent of such feelings yourself. Do you feel no joy at the video clips – so prevalent these days – of American munitions laying waste the structures of your enemies?
But you are at war, you say? Yes, you have a point. I was not at war with America. Far from it: I was the product of an American university; I was earning a lucrative American salary; I was infatuated* with an American woman. So why did part of me desire to see America harmed? I did not know, then; I knew merely that my feelings would be unacceptable to my colleagues, and I undertook to hide them as well as I could. [...]

despicable sickening, repulsive

to compound to make a problem or difficult situation worse
to gloat to be happy about sb. else's failure

infatuated in love with sb. so much that it seems silly

Extract from chapter 11

[On the flight from Santiago to New York] I reflected that I had always resented the manner in which America conducted herself in the world; your country's constant interference in the affairs of others was insufferable* Vietnam, Korea, the straits of Taiwan, the Middle East, and now Afghanistan: in each of the major conflicts and standoffs* that ringed my mother continent of Asia, America played a central role. Moreover I knew from experience as a Pakistani – of alternating periods of American aid and sanctions – that finance was a primary means by which the American empire exercised its power. It was right for me to refuse to participate any longer in facilitating* this project of domination; the only surprise was that I had required so much time to arrive at my decision.

Mohsin Hamid, *The Reluctant Fundamentalist*, Penguin, London 2007, pp. 1–2, 82–84, 177

insufferable extremely unpleasant or annoying
standoff a fight in which neither opponent can do anything to win or achieve their aim

to facilitate to make easier

5. While looking for a suitable definition of "fundamentalism", you probably realized that this term is not restricted to Islamic fundamentalism, but broadly describes any (religious) movement characterized by rigid adherence to certain principles and intolerance of diverging views. Have a look at the photograph and the cartoon. The photo depicts a young member of Westboro Baptist Church campaigning

against homosexuals. Do further research on Westboro Baptist Church and discuss whether its parishioners are fundamentalists.

M4 Terrorist

John Updike

John Updike's novel *Terrorist* tells the story of the American-born Muslim teenager Ahmad who strongly leans towards Islamist-fundamentalist ideologies, despite living in a rather secular environment in the fictitious town of New Prospect.

1. **Point out** what Ahmad is appalled by in his environment.
2. **Characterize** Ahmad and the way he is presented in the text. Consider narrative perspective, Ahmad's train of thought as well as imagery employed by the author.
3. Put yourself in the shoes of Dr. Hamid (cf. **M2**). Prepare a short speech in which you **justify** why Ahmad is a typical "crusader" terrorist, according to the categorization of Hacker (cf. **M1**). Also refer to your own (that is, Dr. Hamid's) experiences.

Devils, Ahmad thinks. *These devils seek to take away my God.* All day long, at Central High School, girls sway* and sneer* and expose their soft bodies and alluring* hair. [...] The teachers, weak Christians and non-observant Jews, make a show of their teaching virtue and righteous* self-restraint, but their shifty eyes and hollow voices betray their lack of belief. They are paid to say these things, by the city of New Prospect and the state of New Jersey. They lack true faith; they are not on the Straight Path; they are unclean. [...] Infidels, they think safety lies in accumulation of the things of this world, and in the corrupting diversion of the television set. They are slaves to images, false ones of happiness and affluence*. But even true images are sinful imitations of God, who can alone create. [...] Their lives away from school are disorderly and wanton* and self-indulgent*. They are paid to instill virtue and democratic values by the state government down in Trenton, and that Satanic government farther down, in Washington, but the values they believe in are Godless: biology and chemistry and physics. [...]

Ahmad is eighteen. This is early April; again green sneaks, seed by seed, into the drab* city's earthy crevices*. He looks down from his new height and thinks that to the insects

to sway to swing gently from side to side
to sneer to speak in a disrespectful manner
alluring attractive and exciting
righteous morally good or correct

affluent rich enough to buy things for pleasure
wanton behaving in a very immoral way
self-indulgent pleasure-seeking

drab not colourful

crevice a narrow crack in a wall or rock

unseen in the grass he would be, if they had a consciousness like his, God. In the past year he has grown three inches, to six feet – more unseen materialistic forces, working their will upon him. He will not grow any taller, he thinks, in this life or the next. If there is a next, an inner devil murmurs. What evidence beyond the prophet's blazing and divinely inspired words proves that there is a next? Where would it be hidden? Who would forever stoke* Hell's boilers? What infinite source of energy would maintain opulent Eden, feeding its dark-eyed houris*, swelling its heavy-hanging fruits, renewing the streams and splashing fountains in which God, as described in the ninth sura of the Qur'an, takes eternal good pleasure? What of the second law of thermodynamics? [...]
Ahmad's teacher, Shaikh Rashid, the imam at the mosque upstairs at $2781\,^1/_2$ West Main Street, [...] is not much older than Ahmad – perhaps ten years, perhaps twenty. He has few wrinkles in the white skin of his face. He is diffident* though precise in his movements. In the years by which he is older, the world has weakened him. When the murmuring of the devils gnawing within him tinges* the imam's voice, Ahmad feels in his own self a desire to rise up and crush him [...]. The student's faith exceeds the master's; it frightens Shaikh Rashid to be riding the winged steed* of Islam, its irresistible onrushing. He seeks to soften the Prophet's words, to make them blend with human reason, but they were not meant to blend: they invade our human softness like a sword. Allah is sublime* beyond all particulars. There is no God but He, the Living, the Self-Subsistent; He is the light by which the sun looks black. He does not blend with our reason but makes our reason bow low, its forehead scraping the dust and bearing like Cain the mark of that dust. Mohammed was a mortal man but visited Paradise and consorted* with the realities there. Our deeds and thoughts were written in the Prophet's consciousness in letters of gold, like the burning words of electrons that a computer creates of pixels as we tap the keyboard.

John Updike, *Terrorist*, Ballantine Books, New York 2006, pp. 1 – 5

to stoke to add fuel to a fire
houris one of the beautiful virgins of the Koranic paradise

diffident shy

to tinge to colour

steed a horse that sb. rides
sublime extremely good or beautiful

to consort to spend time with sb. who is considered bad

Jeff Dunham with Achmed, the Dead Terrorist

Netcode 40650-001

M 5a Achmed, the Dead Terrorist

Jeff Dunham

Jeff Dunham is a ventriloquist (*Bauchredner*) who became especially famous for his ventriloquist's dummy Achmed, the Dead Terrorist, and his exclamation "Silence! I kill you!" When asked why he believed Achmed to be the character that resonated most on *YouTube* by *Time Out* magazine, Dunham responded as follows:

There's an unspoken rule that those characters can go further than the average human can. Maybe it's because people know it's not real. But I think with him in particular, I'm dealing with a subject matter that was kind of taboo ... frightening. As humans we like to laugh at our fears, we like to whistle in the dark. I'm not trying to make fun of anybody who's religious and I do make it a point in every show that Achmed is not Muslim, he's nondescript*. It's just kind of, he's from over there somewhere. But I have heard that even Iraqi businessmen sit around and say "I kill you" to each other and they laugh. And that's some sort of strange compliment to me, I guess, that these guys find it funny as well. Let's all hold hands and sing, "We Are the World"!

Tim Arthur, "Jeff Dunham: Interview", www.timeout.com, 19.04.2010 (06.09.2012)

nondescript very ordinary and not interesting or attractive

M 5b Comedian Defends 'Achmed, the Dead Terrorist' Puppet Routine against South African Ban

Joshua Rhett Miller

In 2008, South Africa banned a ringtone advertisement based on Dunham's show on the grounds that it allegedly mocks Islam. The following article taken from *foxnews.com* describes Dunham's reaction to the South-African ban.

1. **Present** the conflict over Dunham's ringtone advertisement in South Africa.
2. Write a letter to Jeff Dunham in which you comment on the appropriateness of his dealing with the subject matter. Also take into account what Dunham said in the interview with *Time Out* magazine.

It's no laughing matter.

Funnyman ventriloquist Jeff Dunham is fuming after a ringtone advertisement based on his popular comedy skit, "Achmed, the Dead Terrorist," was scrubbed from South African TV because it mocks Islam.

The ringtone was taken from a puppet routine performed by Dunham, a native Texan, in a TV special on Comedy Central. A 10-minute clip of the comedian's routine that was posted on YouTube has been viewed more than 66 million times since April.

But the government of South Africa doesn't think it's funny. According to iafrica.com, South Africa's Advertising Standards Authority (ASA) ruled that a GloMobile ringtone commercial featuring Dunham and his puppet was offensive to Muslims.

The commercial depicts Dunham holding his skeletal puppet, Achmed, dressed with a white cloth around his head and demanding that the audience keep quiet, uttering, "Silence! I will kill you!"

ASA officials said a South African man, Moegamat Khan, had filed a complaint that the commercial was offensive to the Islamic religion and created an impression that all Muslims were terrorists.

And the ASA agreed. "To associate this divine inspiration to a terrorist is offensive to the people who believe in [Muhammad]," the authority ruled. Muslims make up 2 percent of South Africa's population.

But Dunham begs to differ. In a statement to FOXNews.com, he said: "Achmed makes it clear in my act that he is not Muslim, so I'm sorry the gentleman Khan didn't see my entire show.

I've skewered* whites, blacks, Hispanics, Christians, Jews, Muslims, gays, straights, rednecks*, addicts, the elderly, and my wife. As a stand-up comic, it is my job to make the majority of people laugh, and I believe that comedy is the last true form of free speech."

Dunham – whose other puppets include Peanut, Bubba J and Walter, a grumpy retiree – said he has no plans to retire the controversial act.

The comedian said moves like this stymie* the freedom to poke fun at any group.

"I truly believe that laughter can heal many wounds," Dunham said.

In a jibe* at the South African complainant's name, he said: "I thought Khan was awesome in Star Trek."

"If it would help things," he added, "I'm considering renaming Achmed, 'Bill.'"

Joshua Rhett Miller, "Comedian Defends 'Achmed, the Dead Terrorist' Puppet Routine against South African Ban", www.foxnews.com, 02.10.2008 [10.09.2012]

to skewer to push a pointed object into sb., making a hole or causing injury (here: fig.)
redneck a working-class white person from the southern US, especially one who is not educated and does not like people who are not white
to stymie ['staimi] to hold back
jibe a comment that is intended to annoy or offend sb.

M 6 Incendiary

Chris Cleave

After her four-year-old son and husband are killed in a massive suicide bomb attack at a soccer match in London, a distraught woman writes a letter to Osama bin Laden, unaware that this bombing was just the beginning of a series of terror attacks.

1. According to the Macmillan Dictionary, "incendiary" is defined as either "designed for the purpose of causing fire" or "likely to cause anger or violence". After reading the introduction to the text, which of the two definitions might make more sense in the context of the novel?

2. **Point out** how the woman tries to prevent more "boy-shaped holes in the world". (l. 28)

3. **Analyse** by which means the author Chris Cleave makes this text very touching for the reader. Consider narrative perspective, imagery and language. Do not forget to apply the TEE-technique in your analysis (cf. p. 69, AFB II: Analysis).

4. The following quotation is taken from the script of *Incendiary*, a 2008 movie featuring Michelle Williams as the distraught mother:
"I wonder, did you celebrate when you heard my boys got killed? Did you turn on the radio and hear them say a thousand and three dead? Did you put down your mouth over the rocks and kneel down to pray? I prayed. I prayed for the deaths toll to go up to a thousand and four and take me too."
(www.imdb.com/title/tt0984200/quotes; 04.04.2012)
Evaluate whether the director has successfully transformed the character from novel to film.

Dear Osama they want you dead or alive so the terror will stop. Well I wouldn't know about that I mean rock 'n' roll didn't stop when Elvis died on the khazi* it just got worse. Next thing you know there was Sonny & Cher* and Dexys Midnight Runners*. I'll come to them later. My point is it's easier to start these things than to finish them. I suppose you thought of that did you?
There's a reward of 25 million dollars on your head but don't lose sleep on my account Osama. I have no information leading to your arrest or capture. I have no information full effing stop*. I'm what you'd call an infidel* and my husband called working-class. There is a difference you know. But just supposing I did clap eyes on you. Supposing I saw you driving a Nissan Primera down towards Shoreditch* and grassed you to the old bill*. Well, I wouldn't know how to spend 25 million dollars. It's not as if I've got anyone to spend it on since you blew up my husband and my boy.
That's my whole point you see. I don't want 25 million dollars Osama I just want you to give it a rest. AM I ALONE? I want to be the last mother in the world who ever has to write you a letter like this. Who ever has to write to you Osama about her dead boy.
Now about the writing. The last thing I wrote was N/A* on an income support form that wanted NAME OF SPOUSE* OR PARTNER. So you see I'll do my best but you'll have to bear with me because I'm not a big writer. I'm going to write to you about the emptiness that was left when you took my boy away. I'm going to write so you can look into my empty life and see what a human boy really is from the shape of the hole he leaves behind. I want you to feel that hole in your heart and stroke it with your hands and cut your fingers

khazi Cockney (form of English spoken by working-class Londoners) word for toilet
Sonny & Cher an American pop duo in the 1960s and 1970s
Dexys Midnight Runners a British pop group in the early to mid 1980s
full effing stop used in spoken English to emphasize a statement
infidel an insult for sb. who has no religious beliefs or has religious beliefs that are different from yours
Shoreditch an area of London within the borough of Hackney
to grass sb. to the old bill (inf.) to turn sb. in to the police
N/A not applicable/available
spouse a husband, or a wife

on its sharp edges. I am a mother Osama I just want you to love my son. What could be more natural?

I know you can love my boy Osama. The Sun* says you are an EVIL MONSTER but I don't believe in evil I know it takes 2 to tango. I know you're vexed* at the leaders of Western imperialism. Well, I'll be writing to them too.

The Sun a British tabloid
to vex to make sb. angry or annoyed

As for you I know you'd stop the bombs in a second if I could make you see my son with all your heart for just one moment. I know you would stop making boy-shaped holes in the world. It would make you too sad. So I will do my best with these words Osama. I suppose you can see they don't come natural to me but I hope this letter reaches you anyway. I hope it finds you before the Americans do otherwise. I'm going to wish I hadn't bothered aren't I?

Well Osama if I'm going to show you my boy I have to start with where he lived and I still do. I live in London England which I agree with you is a bad place in lots of ways but I was born here so what can you do? London looks like a rich place from the outside but we are most of us very poor here. I saw the video you made Osama where you said the West was decadent. Maybe you meant the West End? We aren't all like that. London is a smiling liar his front teeth are very nice but you can smell his back teeth rotten and stinking.

My family was never rotten poor we were hard up there's a difference. We were respectable we kept ourselves presentable but it was a struggle I don't mind telling you. We were not the nice front teeth or the rotten back teeth of London and there are millions of us just like that. The middle classes put up websites about us. If you're interested Osama just put down that Kalashnikov for a second and look up chav pikey ned* or townie* in Google. Like I say there are millions of us but now there's a lot less than there were of course. I miss them so bad my husband and my boy especially.

Chris Cleave, *Incendiary*, Knopf, New York 2005, pp. 3 f.

chav pikey ned pejorative slang words to refer to people of low social class
townie an urban youth or a form of chav (see above)

5. Against the backdrop of the given text, **discuss** which of the two book covers provided below fits better. Give examples from the text to back up your opinion.

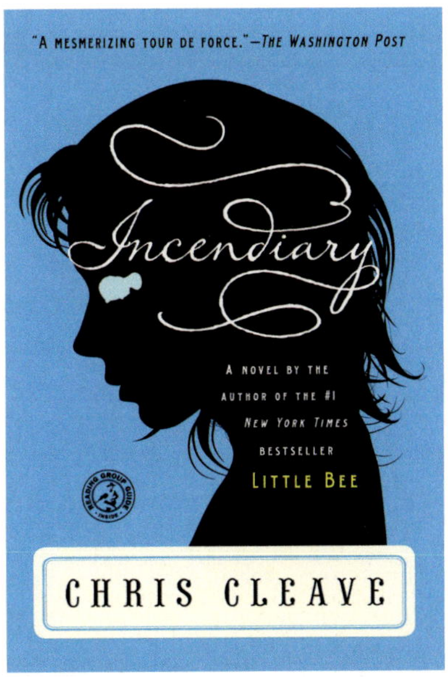

ZOOM IN: Vocabulary

Scherenschnitt silhouette • **verschnörkelt** squiggly

The Sky Is Falling – The 9/11 Attacks

M1 Immediate Reaction in Pictures

During the 9/11 attacks, President George W. Bush was visiting an elementary school where he was listening to a story read by the children. When the second plane hit the World Trade Center, he was informed about the attacks in the midst of the lesson, at 9:06 A.M. Still, he continued listening to the story and left the classroom a few minutes before the scheduled time of 9:20 A.M.

Evaluate Bush's immediate reaction to the 9/11 attacks. What speaks for, what speaks against reacting this way?

Zoom in: Vocabulary

entgeistert aghast, flabbergasted • **nachdenklich** thoughtful • **unentschlossen** undecided

Zoom in: People

George W. Bush

George W. Bush

After having been governor of Texas since 1994, George Walker Bush was elected president on 20 January 2000. He is the son of former US president George Bush Sr. (1989 – 1993) who strongly supported Germany's reunification in 1989. Moreover, Bush Sr. sent American troops to Kuwait after the Iraqi dictator Saddam Hussein had invaded its neighbour state in the summer of 1990.
Like his father, Bush is a member of the Republican Party and favours a strong military. In his first months in office, Bush was rather inconspicuous, which changed after the 9/11 attacks. His immediate action was to declare a War on Terrorism, which included the invasion of Afghanistan in October 2001 since Bush assumed that the Afghan Taliban regime supported Osama bin Laden. This and the later invasion of Iraq in March 2003 (Bush believed that Saddam Hussein possessed weapons of mass destruction which might be used to attack the US) contributed to what became known as the Bush Doctrine: Bush's strategy of preemptively attacking potential enemies.
With regard to domestic policy, Bush was able to implement measures which consisted of stricter security checks at airports and the Patriot Act, which limited Americans' civil rights.

M 2 Broadcast on Qatar's Al-Jazeera TV

Osama bin Laden

The following remarks about the 9/11 attacks by former al Qaeda leader Osama bin Laden were broadcasted on Al-Jazeera TV on 7 October 2001.

Have a close look at the screenshot taken from Osama bin Laden's broadcast. Speculate about its intention. Which impression do you get? Pay special attention to bin Laden's clothes, his facial expression and the background.

Zoom in: Vocabulary

Tarnanzug camouflage jacket • **Turban** turban • **Maschinengewehr** machine gun • **entschlossen** determined

Osama bin Laden

1. **Outline** bin Laden's message.
2. **Explain** how bin Laden justifies the 9/11 attacks and which outlook he gives for the future.

[...] There is America, hit by God in one of its softest spots. Its greatest buildings were destroyed, thank God for that. There is America, full of fear from its north to its south, from its west to its east. Thank God for that.

What America is tasting now is something insignificant compared to what we have tasted for scores of years. Our nation [the Islamic world] has been tasting this humiliation and this degradation for more than 80 years. Its sons are killed, its blood is shed, its sanctuaries* are attacked, and no one hears and no one heeds*. [...]

Bush and those with him [...] have come out in force with their men and have turned even the countries that belong to Islam to this treachery*, and they want to wag their tail at* God, to fight Islam, to suppress people in the name of terrorism. [...]

These events have divided the world into two sides. The side of the believers and the side of infidels, may God keep you away from them. Every Muslim has to rush to make his religion victorious. The winds of faith have come. The winds of change have come to eradicate* oppression from the island of Muhammad, peace be upon him.

To America, I say only a few words to it and its people. I swear by God, [...] neither America nor the people who live in it will dream of security before we live it in Palestine, and not before all the infidel armies leave the land of Muhammad [...].

Osama bin Laden, Broadcast on Al-Jazeera TV, from: www.september11news.com, as reported by USATODAY.com on October 7, 2001, © Associated Press

sanctuary a safe place, especially one where people who are being chased or attacked can stay and be protected
to heed to take notice of
treachery ['tretʃəri] disloyalty
to wag one's tail at sb. to try desperately to get on sb.'s good side
to eradicate to get rid of sth. completely, especially sth. bad

M3 The Falling Man

Richard Drew

The photograph "The Falling Man" taken by Richard Drew is one of the most shocking and vividly remembered pictures of 9/11, capturing the moment a man caught in the upper floors of the World Trade Center either fell when searching for safety, or jumped in order to escape the smoke and the fire. More than 200 people met this fate on 9/11, but the identity of the man depicted in the picture remains unknown up to today. Although the impression is created that he is falling straight down, this picture is in fact part of a series of photographs which, when viewed with the others, shows that the man is actually tumbling through the air.

How does the photograph make you feel? How might the man depicted have felt? Make use of the language support provided.

Zoom in: Vocabulary

beunruhigend disturbing • **scheinbare Ruhe** seeming calmness • **Friedlichkeit** peacefulness • **Dissonanz** dissonance • **Schicksal** fate • **Hoffnungslosigkeit** despair, hopelessness, desperation • **keine Wahl haben** to have no choice

M 4 A Phone Call from the 105th Floor

Beverly Eckert

This account of a good-bye from the 105th floor of the World Trade Center was told by Beverly Eckert, whose husband Sean Rooney worked at Aon in the second tower. Beverly Eckert died in a plane crash in 2009.

1. **Present** the situation Sean Rooney finds himself in and **outline** how this situation deteriorates while talking to his wife on the phone.

2. With reference to the text, **discuss** whether jumping out of the building like the "Falling Man" probably did would have been an option for Sean Rooney (cf. **M3**).

It was about 9:30 a.m. when he called. When I heard his voice on the phone, I was so happy. I said, 'Sean, where are you?,' thinking that he had made it out and that he was calling me from the street somewhere. He told me he was on the 105th floor, and I knew right away that Sean was never coming home. He was very calm. He told me he had been trying to find a way out and what he wanted was information. So I relayed* to him what I could see on TV, what floor the flames had reached and on what side of the building. I also used my other phone, my cell phone, and called 911 and told them where Sean was and that he needed to be rescued. Sean told me that initially he was with some people that tried to escape by going down the stairs, but they had to turn back because of the smoke and the heat. They headed for the roof, but when they got there, they found that the roof doors were locked. He told me the other people were now in a conference room and that he was alone. I asked him to go back and try the roof doors again, to pound on them, and that somebody on the other side would hear him ... Sean was gone for maybe five minutes, and then he came back to the phone. He hadn't had any success, and now the stairwell was full of smoke: He had actually passed out for a few minutes while pounding on the doors. There was a building in flames underneath him, but Sean didn't even flinch*. He stayed composed, just talking to me the way he always did. I will always be in awe of the way he faced death. Not an ounce of fear – not when the windows around him were getting too hot to touch; not when the smoke was making it hard to breathe. By now we had stopped talking about escape routes. I wanted to use the precious few minutes we had left just to talk. He told me to give his love to his family, and then we just began talking about all the happiness we shared during our lives together, how lucky we were to have each other. At one point, when I could tell it was getting harder for him to breathe, I asked if it hurt. He paused for a moment, and then said, 'No.' He loved me enough to lie. In the end, as the smoke got thicker, he just kept whispering, 'I love you,' over and over. Then I suddenly heard this loud explosion through the phone. It reverberated* for several seconds. We held our breath; I know we both realized what was about to happen. Then I heard a sharp crack, followed by the sound of an avalanche*. I heard Sean gasp once as the floor fell out from underneath him. I called his name into the phone over and over. Then I just sat there huddled on the floor holding the phone to my heart.

"Good-Bye. A phone call from the 105th floor", http://nymag.com, 27.08.2011 [06.09.2012]

to relay to communicate information to sb.

to not flinch to remain calm despite anger or shock

to reverberate to shake slightly because of a loud sound that is repeated many times

avalanche a large amount of a substance that falls somewhere

3. Try to put yourself in the shoes of the "Falling Man", calling his family before he jumps out of the building. What would he tell them? Write their telephone conversation, with reference to Sean Rooney's account of the circumstances within the building.

M5 Gelato Is Gelato

Jennifer Belle

Jennifer Belle is a best-selling American author who has also written for *New York Magazine* and *People* magazine. She lives in Greenwich Village, a large residential neighbourhood on the west side of Lower Manhattan in New York City. In the given excerpt, she reports about her Weight Watchers meetings shortly after the 9/11 attacks. Weight Watchers is a commercial weight-loss programme based on calorie and portion control, calculated in a certain number of points a person is allowed to each day.

1. "Weight Watchers believes that dieting is just one part of long-term weight management. A healthy body results from a healthy lifestyle – which means mental, emotional, and physical health. Weight Watchers does not tell people what they can or can't eat. The goal is to help people make healthy eating decisions and encourage them to enjoy more physical activity, thereby losing weight safely and sensibly. At local group meetings, Weight Watchers members get motivation, mutual support, and encouragement in handling the challenges encountered in the process of changing behavior."

   "Weight Watchers", www.medicinenet.com [06.09.2012]

   Against the backdrop of the Weight Watchers philosophy provided above, make an educated guess on the connection between 9/11 and the title of this excerpt.

2. **State** the different ways the people in the excerpt cope with 9/11.

3. **Characterize** Estelle and the way she is presented in the text.

4. **Examine** how the two Weight Watchers meetings differ from each other as well as the different strategies employed to cope with 9/11.

5. **Comment** on the appropriateness of Estelle's statement that she "never thought [they'd] see another holocaust". (l. 48)

brooch a piece of jewellery with a pin on the back that you fasten to your clothes
easel a frame used for supporting a paper or board

shrink (inf.) psychiatrist

Estelle stood at the front of the room in her black pants outfit with her signature brooch* – a different one every week sparkling at her ample breast. "Hello I'm Estelle" was written in red magic marker on her giant pad standing on its easel*. Her big square hands with their girlish diamond engagement ring were clasped together.
It was September 18, one week since the World Trade Center had gone down.
"Are there any new members joining today?" Estelle asked in her Jewish New York accent. No hands went up. Estelle looked very grave.
I had just come from therapy where my shrink* said that the people who jumped from the towers were in an out of body state, a state of ecstasy, drugged from adrenaline, not in a regular state, not in a state that we could ever understand. As they jumped, they might have even thought they could fly. I was deeply comforted.
One by one the women in the group raised their hands and said how much weight they'd gained since September 11. Two pounds, three pounds, five pounds, eight pounds. Rounding down, I had gained three myself. Not in a regular state.
Estelle had been a leader for over thirty years. She was over seventy years old. She had maintained a "realistic goal weight" – meaning, she was fat but she thought she was thin. I loved Estelle. She was the personification of everything I wanted to be when I was her age. She was blonde. She had a good body-image. She was wildly in love with her husband. She took pride in controlling her portions.

I had never seen Estelle so serious. In all her years, she had never faced a Weight Watchers crisis like this one.

When the last person had spoken, Estelle remained silent for a fewmoments. Finally she spoke.

"A bagel is a bagel," she said.

Everyone sat, transfixed*.

"And gelato is just gelato."

A few people started slowly nodding.

"And ice cream is just ice cream, and a cake is just a cake, and a hamburger is just a hamburger, and French fries are just French fries, and a bag of Pirate's Booty* is just a bag of Pirate's Booty ..."

"And I ate them all," I said without thinking. Everybody laughed causing me to flush with pleasure.

"Good!" she said. "If it makes you feel better – eat!" We all sat there stunned.

"What's wrong with eating? If you come to my house right now you'll find every kind of ice cream and cookie there is."

I was shocked. This was too much information. She had told us what she ate for breakfast every morning – 1/2 cup bran cereal, 1 cup skim milk, 1/2 cup blueberries. She had told us that she had gotten rid of all her dinner plates and replaced them with salad plates so that her portions would appear bigger. [...] But she had never given us such a complete look into her refrigerator before. Opened her cupboards up wide. Estelle was our leader. I revered* her, to the point of worship. And now she was standing naked and vulnerable before us.

"Really," Estelle insisted, "come to my house right now. I have enough kinds of ice cream so every one of you could take your pick. Does anyone here like brownies?"

There were gasps. It was anarchy. [...]

"Eat!" she said. "Do whatever it takes to make yourselves feel better." Someone laughed nervously.

"In my lifetime," she said, "I never thought we'd see another holocaust."

I stayed in bed the rest of the week eating and watching television. A week was just a week. A chip was just a chip. I couldn't wait to go back to Weight Watchers and weigh in. A pound was a pound. Two pounds were two pounds. A state of ecstasy.

But when I went back to Weight Watchers the old Estelle was back. The anarchy had ended. But we wouldn't ever be the same. Estelle had said, "Eat!" and for a moment I had known what it felt like to be completely free, to be thin, to fly.

It was like Hitler opening the camp gates. It was like my shrink telling me to just go ahead and kill my parents.

"Think of all the people who died in the towers who were on Weight Watchers, working hard to follow the plan, keeping track of their points," Estelle said. I imagined a secretary whose last meal was a Just 2 Points Bar. "They would have wanted us to stay on the program," one woman said, wiping tears from her eyes.

"Do it for them," Estelle said.

Jennifer Belle, "Gelato is Gelato", in: Ulrich Baer (ed.), *110 Stories. New York writes after September 11*, New York University Press, New York/London 2002, pp. 37 – 39

transfixed so surprised or shocked that you continue to look or listen without moving

Pirate's Booty a puffed rice and corn snack

to revere [rɪˈvɪə(r)] to have a lot of respect and admiration for sb.

M 6 Address to the Nation: September 11, 2001

George W. Bush

In reaction to the 9/11 attacks, then-President George W. Bush delivered an address to the nation.

1. In his speech, Bush makes use of a quotation from the Bible, namely Psalm 23, which says: *Even though I walk through the valley of the shadow of death, I fear no evil for you are with me.* Relate the quotation to the 9/11 attacks and make an educated guess on the message Bush is trying to convey in his speech.

Netcode 40650-002

Listening

2. **Compare** the basic ideas expressed and the rhetoric employed in this speech with Bush's immediate reaction to the attacks, as captured in the pictures provided in **M1**. Think of reasons for similarities or differences.

M 7 Policy Statement on the 9/11 Attacks

Gerhard Schröder

One day after the attacks on the World Trade Center in New York, German chancellor Gerhard Schröder (SPD) gave this policy statement in the German *Bundestag* on 12 September 2001 as Germany's official reaction to the USA having been attacked.

ZOOM IN: People

Gerhard Schröder

Gerhard Schröder (l.) in a conversation with George W. Bush

Gerhard Schröder was German chancellor from 1998 to 2005. He is a member of the Social Democratic Party (SPD) and was minister president in Lower Saxony from 1990 to 1998.
Schröder's reaction after the 9/11 attacks included unrestricted solidarity with the US which would have meant Germany's military involvement in the War on Terrorism. However, the German *Bundestag* rejected any kind of military involvement and thus Schröder had no other choice than to ask for a vote of confidence in order to support the US in Operation Enduring Freedom. However, the USA's fight against Iraq was supported by neither Schröder nor by the German public, which explicitly voiced its anti-war attitude in several demonstrations. Schröder's opposition to the Iraq invasion helped him win the elections in 2002. This position led to tensions with the US government. Nevertheless, Schröder was criticized for having supported the Iraq war indirectly since German intelligence provided the US with information about possible targets in Iraq's capital Baghdad.

1. Imagine there is an American exchange student in your English class. He/she is interested in Germany's immediate reaction to 9/11, but is not able to fully understand German yet. Briefly **outline** the gist of Schröder's policy statement. Focus on his concept of "unrestricted solidarity" (ll. 26f.).

2. **Compare** Schröder's policy statement with Bush's address to the nation delivered on September 11, 2001 in regards to content and rhetoric. Think of reasons for similarities as well as differences.

Herr Präsident! Meine sehr verehrten Damen und Herren! Der gestrige 11. September 2001 wird als ein schwarzer Tag für uns alle in die Geschichte eingehen. Noch heute sind wir fassungslos* angesichts eines nie da gewesenen Terroranschlags auf das, was unsere Welt im Innersten zusammenhält.

Wir wissen noch nicht, wer hinter dieser Kriegserklärung an die zivilisierte Völkergemeinschaft steht. Wir wissen noch nicht einmal, wie viel Tausende ganz und gar unschuldige Menschen den feigen* Attentaten zum Opfer gefallen sind. Wir wissen und erfahren aber: Jetzt geht es darum, unser Mitgefühl*, unsere Solidarität zu zeigen: Solidarität mit der Bevölkerung der Vereinigten Staaten von Amerika, und zwar Solidarität aller, die für Frieden und Freiheit einstehen, in Deutschland, in Europa, überall auf der Welt.

2000 Menschen haben sich gestern Abend zu einer spontanen Beileidskundgebung* und zu einem Gottesdienst im Berliner Dom versammelt. Im Anschluss an diese Sitzung des Deutschen Bundestages wird ein ökumenischer* Trauergottesdienst in der Sankt-Hedwigs-Kathedrale stattfinden.

Der Deutsche Gewerkschaftsbund* und die Bundesvereinigung der Deutschen Arbeitgeberverbände* haben dazu aufgerufen, am Donnerstag um 10 Uhr für fünf Minuten in der Arbeit innezuhalten. Die Bundesregierung wird diesem Aufruf für die Institutionen des Bundes folgen.

Meine Damen und Herren, ich habe dem amerikanischen Präsidenten das tief empfundene Beileid* des gesamten deutschen Volkes ausgesprochen. Ich habe ihm auch die uneingeschränkte* – ich betone: die uneingeschränkte – Solidarität Deutschlands zugesichert*. Ich bin sicher, unser aller Gedanken sind bei den Opfern und ihren Angehörigen. Ihnen gilt unser Mitgefühl, unsere ganze Anteilnahme*.

Ich möchte hier in Anwesenheit des neuen amerikanischen Botschafters Dan Coates noch einmal ausdrücklich versichern: Die Menschen in Deutschland stehen in dieser schweren Stunde fest an der Seite der Vereinigten Staaten von Amerika.

(Beifall im ganzen Hause)

Selbstverständlich bieten wir den Bürgern und Behörden der Vereinigten Staaten von Amerika jede gewünschte Hilfe an, natürlich auch bei der Ermittlung und Verfolgung der Urheber und Drahtzieher* dieser niederträchtigen* Attentate.

Bei meinem Gespräch mit den Partei- und Fraktionsvorsitzenden* am gestrigen Abend bestand völlige Einmütigkeit* darüber, dass diese außergewöhnliche Situation das Zusammenstehen aller Demokraten erfordert. Die gestrigen Anschläge in New York und Washington sind nicht nur ein Angriff auf die Vereinigten Staaten von Amerika; sie sind eine Kriegserklärung gegen die gesamte zivilisierte Welt. Diese Art von terroristischer Gewalt, das wahllose Auslöschen unschuldiger Menschenleben stellt die Grundregeln unserer Zivilisation infrage. Sie bedroht unmittelbar die Prinzipien menschlichen Zusammenlebens in Freiheit und Sicherheit, all das also, was in Generationen aufgebaut wurde. Gemeinsam werden wir diese Werte – sei es in Amerika, sei es in Europa oder wo auch immer in der Welt – nicht zerstören lassen.

fassungslos stunned

feige cowardly
Mitgefühl compassion, sympathy

Beileidskundgebung demonstration of condolence
ökumenisch ecumenical [ˌiːkjʊˈmenɪk(ə)l]
Gewerkschaftsbund federation of trade unions
Arbeitgeberverband employers' federation

Beileid condolence
uneingeschränkt unrestricted
zusichern to assure
Anteilnahme sympathy

Drahtzieher wirepuller
niederträchtig malicious
Parteivorsitzende/r party leader
Fraktionsvorsitzende/r chairperson of a parliamentary group
Einmütigkeit unanimity

Memorial Service at the Brandenburg Gate in Berlin for the victims of 9/11, 14 September 2001, attended by around 200,000 people.

In Wirklichkeit – das zeigt sich immer mehr – sind wir bereits eine Welt. Deshalb sind die Anschläge in New York, dem Sitz der Vereinten Nationen, und in Washington gegen uns alle gerichtet. Der gestrige terroristische Angriff hat uns noch einmal vor Augen geführt: Sicherheit ist in unserer Welt nicht teilbar*. Sie ist nur zu erreichen, wenn wir noch enger für unsere Werte zusammenstehen und bei ihrer Durchsetzung zusammenarbeiten.

nicht teilbar indivisible

Wir müssen nun rasch noch wirksamere Maßnahmen* ergreifen, um dem Terrorismus weltweit den Nährboden zu entziehen*. Es hat zu gelten: Wer Terroristen hilft oder sie schützt, verstößt gegen alle fundamentalen Werte des Zusammenlebens der Völker. Ich habe noch gestern Abend mit dem französischen Staatspräsidenten Chirac und Ministerpräsident Jospin, mit dem britischen Premierminister Blair und dem russischen Präsidenten Putin gesprochen. Wir sind uns in der Bewertung* einig, dass diese Terrorakte eine Kriegserklärung an die freie Welt bedeuten.

wirksame Maßnahmen active measures
den Nährboden entziehen to take away the breeding ground

Bewertung assessment

Die Außenminister der Europäischen Union werden noch heute zu einer Sondersitzung zusammentreten. Danach wird es notwendig sein, dass die Europäische Union auf höchster Ebene* ihre Solidarität zum Ausdruck bringt. Ich habe den amtierenden Ratspräsidenten* der Europäischen Union, den belgischen Ministerpräsidenten Verhofstadt, gebeten, eine entsprechende Initiative zu ergreifen.

auf höchste Ebene at the highest level
Ratspräsident President of the Council of the European Union

Viele Menschen werden sich fragen: Was bedeuten diese Anschläge für uns in Deutschland? Ich habe gestern Abend unverzüglich eine Sitzung des Bundessicherheitsrates* einberufen. Wir haben auf der Grundlage der uns zugänglichen Informationen die Lage eingehend analysiert. Derzeit liegen keine Hinweise auf eine außerordentliche* Bedrohung der Sicherheit unseres Landes vor. Gleichwohl haben wir zusätzliche Maßnahmen ergriffen*, die zum Schutz der Menschen in unserem Land erforderlich sind. Das betrifft insbesondere die Sicherheit des Luftraums* und des Flugverkehrs sowie den Schutz amerikanischer und anderer herausgehobener Einrichtungen.

Bundessicherheitsrat federal security council

außerordentlich extraordinary
Maßnahmen ergreifen to take measures
Luftraum air space

Darüber hinaus werden wir gemeinsam überlegen müssen, welche längerfristigen Konsequenzen aus diesen fürchterlichen Anschlägen zu ziehen sind. Der Bundessicherheitsrat wird heute Vormittag zu einer erneuten Sitzung zusammenkommen. Es ist selbstverständlich, dass wir alle Fraktionen des Deutschen Bundestages, die Vorsitzenden der politischen Parteien, aber auch die Öffentlichkeit über die weiteren Entwicklungen informieren werden. Die nächste Unterrichtung der Partei- und Fraktionsvorsitzenden erfolgt, wie verabredet, bereits heute Mittag im Bundeskanzleramt.

Ich bin davon überzeugt: Gemeinsam werden wir uns dieser verbrecherischen Herausforderung gewachsen zeigen. Freiheit und Demokratie, die Werte des friedlichen Zusammenlebens der Menschen und der Völker, werden diese Prüfung bestehen.

(Beifall im ganzen Hause)

Regierungserklärung des Bundeskanzlers Gerhard Schröder zu den Anschlägen in den Vereinigten Staaten von Amerika, 12.09.2001, in: www.documentarchiv.de [06.09.2012]

3. 9/11 also affected Germany in various ways. Find out more about Germany and 9/11 with the help of a questionnaire that you yourself design. You could for example ask your parents, other relatives or people you know about how they experienced that day as well as its after-effects. You might want to ask about:

- what they were doing on the day the skyscrapers came down
- how they felt about it
- which images they still remember
- the impact 9/11 had on Germany's domestic as well as foreign policy and your interviewees' stance on this
- ... or anything else you find particularly interesting or worth talking about.

Interpret the data you collected and present your findings to your class. After the presentations, discuss in how far 9/11 changed not only the US, but Germany as well.

ZOOM IN: Skills

How to write good survey questions

- Begin with general questions as a warm-up, followed by more specific questions.
- When using multiple-choice questions, make sure that the answers are mutually exclusive and do not overlap, so that your interviewee can make a clear choice.
- Be specific in what you want to know.
- Avoid difficult words or technical terms to ensure your interviewee's understanding.
- Do not force answers. Some questions might be too intrusive, so be sure to respect your interviewee's privacy.
- Ask only one question at a time.
- Use short and precise questions.

taken and adapted from: "Survey Design: Writing Great Questions for Online Surveys", http://free-questionnaire-templates.esurveyspro.com, 8 October 2008 [06.09.2012]

M 8 Part One of the Speech at the Labour Party Conference

Tony Blair

Like many other heads of government, British Prime Minister Tony Blair elaborated on the 9/11 attacks in a speech he delivered at the Labour Party Conference on 2 October 2001. This is part one of his speech.

ZOOM IN: People

Tony Blair

Tony Blair

Tony Blair (Labour Party) was British Prime Minister from 1997 to 2007. Right from the beginning, Blair completely supported the US in its plans to fight the War on Terrorism even when it became obvious that Bush wanted to attack Iraq in 2003. This position led to heavy quarrels within the European Union since opponents argued that overthrowing a dictatorship was no reason for starting a war. However, the British troops made up one third of the army's complete force level in Iraq.
Soon after the invasion of Iraq it became apparent that the country did not have any weapons of mass destruction and Blair was accused of having exaggerated the Iraqi threat on purpose. This topic is still debated today.

1. **Present** Blair's argumentation.

2. **Illustrate** how Blair tries to convince his fellow party members of his opinion. Which stylistic devices are used in order to appeal to the audience's feelings?

Netcode 40650-003

3. Rehearse the speech for presentation purposes together with a partner. Before you start, have a closer took at the speech again and decide which words, phrases or passages should be emphasized. Like a poem, a speech is only as good as its presenter, so use your voice to put special emphasis on words, for example by lowering your voice, etc.
After thorough rehearsal, present your version in class!

Millennium turn of the century
to clutch to hold close
to implore to beg
memorial remembrance
savagery cruelty
anxious worried
rubble remains of a building

In retrospect, the Millennium* marked only a moment in time. It was the events of September 11 that marked a turning point in history, where we confront the dangers of the future and assess the choices facing humankind.
It was a tragedy. An act of evil. From this nation goes our deepest sympathy and prayers for the victims and our profound solidarity with the American people.
We were with you at the first. We will stay with you to the last.
Just two weeks ago, in New York, after the church service I met some of the families of the British victims.
It was in many ways a very British occasion. Tea and biscuits. It was raining outside. Around the edge of the room, strangers making small talk, trying to be normal people in an abnormal situation.
And as you crossed the room, you felt the longing and sadness; hands clutching* photos of sons and daughters, wives and husbands; imploring* you to believe them when they said there was still an outside chance of their loved ones being found alive, when you knew in truth that all hope was gone.
And then a middle-aged mother looks you in the eyes and tells you her only son has died, and asks you: why?
I tell you: you do not feel like the most powerful person in the country at times like that. Because there is no answer. There is no justification for their pain. Their son did nothing wrong. The woman, seven months pregnant, whose child will never know its father, did nothing wrong.
They don't want revenge. They want something better in memory of their loved ones.
I believe their memorial* can and should be greater than simply the punishment of the guilty. It is that out of the shadow of this evil, should emerge lasting good: destruction of the machinery of terrorism wherever it is found; hope amongst all nations of a new beginning where we seek to resolve differences in a calm and ordered way; greater understanding between nations and between faiths; and above all justice and prosperity for the poor and dispossessed, so that people everywhere can see the chance of a better future through the hard work and creative power of the free citizen, not the violence and savagery* of the fanatic.
I know that here in Britain people are anxious*, even a little frightened. I understand that.
People know we must act but they worry what might follow.
They worry about the economy and talk of recession.
And, of course there are dangers; it is a new situation.
But the fundamentals of the US, British and European economies are strong.
Every reasonable measure of internal security is being undertaken.
Our way of life is a great deal stronger and will last a great deal longer than the actions of fanatics, small in number and now facing a unified world against them.
People should have confidence. This is a battle with only one outcome: our victory not theirs.
What happened on 11 September was without parallel in the bloody history of terrorism.
Within a few hours, up to 7000 people were annihilated, the commercial centre of New York was reduced to rubble* and in Washington and Pennsylvania further death and hor-

ror on an unimaginable scale. Let no one say this was a blow for Islam when the blood of innocent Muslims was shed along with those of the Christian, Jewish and other faiths around the world.
We know those responsible. In Afghanistan are scores* of training camps for the export of terror. Chief amongst the sponsors and organisers is Osama Bin Laden.
He is supported, shielded and given succour* by the Taliban regime.
Two days before the 11 September attacks, Masood, the leader of the opposition Northern Alliance, was assassinated by two suicide bombers. Both were linked to Bin Laden. Some may call that coincidence. I call it payment – payment in the currency these people deal in: blood.
Be in no doubt: Bin Laden and his people organised this atrocity*. The Taliban aid and abet* him. He will not desist* from further acts of terror. They will not stop helping him. Whatever the dangers of the action we take, the dangers of inaction are far, far greater. [...]
"Full Text: Tony Blair's Speech", www.guardian.co.uk, 02.10.2001 [06.09.2012]

scores (pl.) very many

succour ['sʌkə] assistance, help

atrocity barbarity
to abet to assist, to help in wrongdoing
to desist to stop, to refrain from doing sth.

4. Now that you have dealt with three nations' reactions on 9/11, prepare a five-minute talk in which you summarize the American, German and British positions briefly. Elaborate on which speech you found most convincing and give reasons for your choice.

M 9 Recent Tragic Events

Craig Wright

In Craig Wright's philosophical comedy *Recent Tragic Events*, Waverly and Andrew are on a blind date in Minneapolis on the evening of 12 September 2001. In the given excerpt, Andrew has just arrived with a bottle of wine whereas Waverly has desperately been trying to reach her sister in New York.

1. Have a look at the photograph. What does it reveal about the impact of the 9/11 attacks?

2. Despite the attacks, Waverly and Andrew meet for their blind date. With reference to the photograph, **outline** how they both perceived the day before.

3. **Examine** in how far the 9/11 attacks are omnipresent in the characters' conversation, in spite of their efforts to have a "normal" blind date.

4. Write a continuation of the play, in which the fate of Waverly's sister is revealed. You can choose either a happy or a tragic ending. Your continuation should be consistent with the excerpt in regards to language and the way the characters are presented, so consider your findings from tasks 2 and 3.

This photograph shows the site of the attacks on 12 September 2001.

Waverly So can you believe this?

Andrew No, it feels like a weird dream. I was just in New York, like, two weeks ago.

Waverly Really? *(Referring to the World Trade Center.)* Did you know anybody in there?

Andrew I, uh, I don't think so.

Waverly Or on the planes?

Andrew No.

Waverly Or at the Pentagon?

Andrew No.

Waverly Excellent. *(After a beat.)* What are the odds* of that, I wonder. Not knowing anybody?

Andrew Yeah.

Waverly *(A grim joke.)* I mean, this must be a really hard day for Kevin Bacon. *(After a beat.)* You know, because of the ...

Andrew ... the thing*.

Waverly Yeah. *(After a beat.)* So are you from Minneapolis, originally?

Andrew All my life. You?

Waverly Ever since I got out of college. I went to Carleton, down in Northfield?

Andrew Cool.

Waverly You?

Andrew The U.*

Waverly Excellent.

Andrew *(After a beat.)* I keep forgetting about the Pentagon.

Waverly Totally. I remember when I first saw Jim Miklascewski* on NBC, and he was, like, "Wait a second, Katie, I think an explosion just went off nearby," and I was thinking: "Right. You need to relax, Jim." Like, of course, he thinks anywhere something goes boom now, it's gotta be more planes. And then it was! *(She dials the phone again, waits to hear something.)*

Andrew Who're you trying to call? If I can ask?

Waverly My sister. But ... she's not home.
(She hangs up the phone.)
She's kind of a kook* and she's never home and she doesn't have a cell phone. It's very annoying. *(Closing the phone.)* So look, let me dry my hair and get ready and we can go?

Andrew We don't really have to do this, you know ...

Waverly No, I want to, this'll be a relief. I wanna get out of here. I've been going nuts just sitting around. This is good.

Craig Wright, *Recent Tragic Events*, Dramatist's Play Service, New York 2004

odds the chances of something happening

the thing referring to the game *Six Degrees of Kevin Bacon* which is based on the assumption that anyone working in the Hollywood film industry can – via the roles they played – be related to Kevin Bacon in six steps

The U here: University of Minnesota in Minneapolis

Jim Miklascewski the chief Pentagon correspondent for *NBC News* who was reporting live for the *Today Show* when a plane hit the Pentagon, where his office is based. Listen to his report on *YouTube:*

Netcode 40650-004

kook one whose ideas or actions are eccentric, fantastic, or insane

5. In order to stage a play, specific stage directions are needed which tell the actors exactly how to behave or how to speak. Based on your analysis results, write the stage directions for this excerpt from *Recent Tragic Events*. Then stage your version in class.

Zoom in: Skills

How to write stage directions	
1. Scene directions Scene directions start the play or act and include basic information about the setting as well as what is happening when the lights come on, or what has happened between scenes.	**Example:** *A living room. Two armchairs, one toward either side of the stage, facing each other diagonally out toward the audience. Against the rear wall, a sofa. [...] At the beginning,* MOMMY *and* DADDY *are seated in the armchairs,* DADDY *in the armchair stage-left,* MOMMY *in the other. Curtain up.*
2. Staging directions Staging directions describe what happens on stage during the scene, such as who enters or leaves the stage, or light changes.	**Example**: DADDY Watch now; it's opening. *(He opens the door)* It's open! *(MRS. BARKER steps into the room)*
3. Character stage directions Character stage directions should always be short and positioned right under the character's name. They serve to explain the style of a line and should only be used if the reader would not be able to understand the line without them.	**Example:** DADDY *(Tonelessly)* Well, my dear, I know beige from wheat, too.
4. In general: Stage directions are always put in parentheses and italics and should by no means tell about the feelings or thoughts of the characters, since they are only supposed to show what is taking place on stage.	

adapted and taken from: www.scriptfrenzy.org/howtoformatastageplay [10.06.2012]; examples taken from: Edward Albee: "The American Dream"; in: *The American Dream, The Zoo Story. Two Plays by Edward Albee*, Plume Books, New York 1997, pp. 57, 60, 75

M 10 a Aftermath

Meena Alexander

Meena Alexander

Meena Alexander (*1951) is an Indian-born poet and writer who lives in New York City. In the poem *Aftermath*, she describes her perception of 9/11 only a few days after the attacks. The poem *Invisible City* (**M 10 b**) describes her perception a few weeks after the attacks. Split into two groups, one group dealing with **M 10 a**, the other with **M 10 b**. Do tasks 1 and 2 on your own and find a partner who has worked on the other poem for task 3.

1. Reading for gist: **State** in one sentence only how Meena Alexander feels about the 9/11 attacks.

2. **Illustrate** how the poet makes use of imagery and stylistic devices to convey her feelings about the attacks. In order to do so, copy and fill in the missing parts of the T-E-E table. Continue the table with further stylistic devices you find.

T(hesis)	E(xample)	E(xplanation)
The poet frequently makes use of alliterations.	One example can be found in the very last verse of the poem, when the poet states that "smoke stains the sky" (l. 12).	?
In regards to imagery, there are lots of words and phrases taken from the semantic field of nature.	?	Here, nature does not represent something innocent or beautiful any more, but rather stands for destruction, death and decay.
?	The poet speaks about "[s]yllables of flame [which] stitch the rubble" (l.10).	Thus, she illustrates the attempt to stitch what has been broken, even though in this case this attempt seems to be futile or rather unleashes more destruction.

3. Find a partner who has worked on **Text B**, *Invisible City*. Exchange your results and explain in how far **Text B** is a continuation of **Text A**. You could start off by looking for words that are used in both poems and identify their respective contexts, but you should also focus on recurring images as well as stylistic devices.

There is an uncommon light in the sky
Pale petals* are scored into stone.

I want to write of the linden tree
That stoops* at the edge of the river

But its leaves are filled with insects
With wings the color of dry blood.

At the far side of the river Hudson
By the southern tip of our island

A mountain soars*, a torrent* of sentences
Syllables of flame stitch the rubble*

An eye, a lip, a cut hand blooms
Sweet and bitter smoke stains* the sky.

petal one of the coloured parts around the centre of a flower
to stoop to bend, crouch

to soar to rise quickly into the air
torrent a large amount of sth. unpleasant
rubble broken remains of buildings
to stain to damage or spoil

Meena Alexander, "Aftermath", in: Ulrich Baer (ed.), *110 Stories. New York writes after September 11*, New York University Press, New York/London 2002, p. 21

M 10 b Invisible City

Meena Alexander

The poem *Invisible City* describes Meena Alexander's perception of 9/11 not a few days, but a few weeks after the attacks.

1. Reading for gist: **State** in one sentence only how Meena Alexander feels about the 9/11 attacks.

2. Illustrate how the poet makes use of imagery and stylistic devices to convey her feelings about the attacks. In order to do so, copy and fill in the missing parts of the T-E-E table. Continue the table with further stylistic devices you find.

T(hesis)	E(xample)	E(xplanation)
The poet frequently makes use of alliterations.	One example can be found in the very first line of the poem, when the poet states that "smoke stains the air".	?
In regards to imagery, there are lots of words and phrases taken from the semantic field of nature.	?	Here, nature does not represent something innocent or beautiful anymore, but rather stands for destruction, death and decay.
?	The poet speaks about a "thread torn out" (l. 2) and about a "seam of sense" (l. 10).	Thus, she compares the destruction of the towers to tearing apart a piece of clothing. It seems futile to try to mend it again because the damage is so severe.

3. Find a partner who has worked on **Text A** *Aftermath*. Exchange your results and explain in how far **Text B** is a continuation of **Text A**. You could start off by looking for words that are used in both poems and identify their respective contexts, but you should also focus on recurring images as well as stylistic devices.

Sweet and bitter smoke stains* the air
The verb *stains* has a thread* torn out
I step out to the linden grove*
Bruised trees are the color of sand.

Something uncoils* and blows at my feet.
Silver of mist*? Bolt* of beautitude?

A scrap of what was once called sky?
I murmur words that come to me

Tall towers, twin towers I used to see.
A bloody seam* of sense drops free.

By Liberty Street, on a knot of rubble*
In altered light, I see a bird cry.

to stain to damage or spoil
thread [θred] a long thin fibre used for sewing
grove a group of trees of a particular type
to uncoil to become straight after being curled
mist a cloud of very small drops of water in the air just above the ground
bolt *here:* revelation
seam a line of stitches that joins two pieces of cloth
rubble broken remains of buildings

Meena Alexander, "Invisible City", in: Ulrich Baer (ed.), *110 Stories. New York writes after September 11*, New York University Press, New York/London 2002, p. 22

M 11 After 9/11. Stress and Coping Across America

Testimony

Here are some results from a survey conducted by researchers three to five days after the 9/11 attacks. The researchers were interested in finding out how the average American was coping with the trauma. The survey results were then presented to the United States Senate Committee on Health, Education, Labor and Pensions.

Interpret the results with regard to how Americans attempted to cope with 9/11 immediately after the attacks. Then **evaluate** the impact the attacks had on the population, according to this survey.

Some Questions We Asked	
Adults	**Substantial Stress (%)**
Since Tuesday, have you been bothered by:	
Feeling very upset when something reminds you of what happened?	30
Repeated disturbing memories, thoughts, or dreams about what happened?	16
Having difficulty concentrating?	14
Trouble falling or staying asleep?	11
Feeling irritable or having angry outbursts?	9
At least one of the above?	44

(Possible reponses were "not at all," "a little bit," "moderately," "quite a bit" and "extremely." Substantial stress was defined as an answer of "quite a bit" or "extremely.")

Children	
Since Tuesday, has your child been:	
Avoiding talking or hearing about what happened?	18
Having trouble keeping his or her mind on things and concentrating?	12
Having trouble falling or staying asleep?	10
Losing his or her temper or being irritable?	10
Having nightmares?	6
At least one of the above?	35
Worried about his or her safety or the safety of a loved one?	47

(For children, stress was defined as a response of "yes" on a two-point scale ["yes," "no"].)

Zoom in: Vocabulary

Talking about statistics

The bar chart represents ... • The figures can be interpreted as follows. • A high/low percentage of Americans ... • In comparison, adults and children differed in regards to ... • (More than) half of Americans ... • Over two thirds ... • The overwhelming majority/minority ... • Only a few ... • A third of ... • (Roughly) two out of five Americans ... • What is (also) striking is ... • From this one can conclude/deduce ...

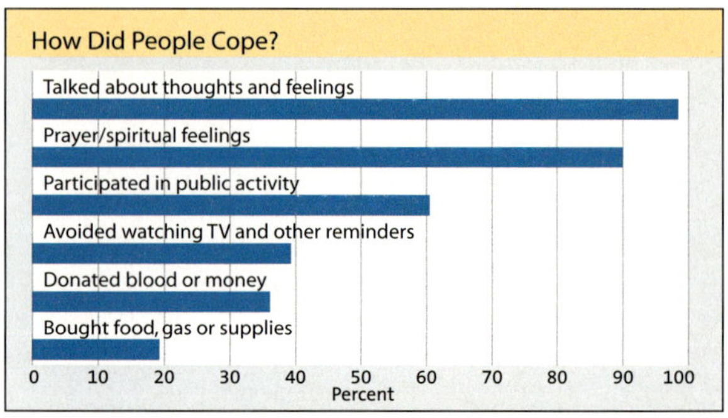

RAND, "After 9/11: Stress and Coping Across America", www.rand.org, 2002 [06.09.2012]

M 12 Conspiracy Theories: Denying the Unbelievable

A conspiracy theory is defined as "a theory that explains an event as being the result of a plot by a covert group or organization; a belief that a particular unexplained event was caused by such a group" [http://dictionary.reference.com/browse/conspiracy+theory]. Especially after 9/11, conspiracy theories became widely popular and spread among the American population and beyond.

1. Make an educated guess on why people tend to believe conspiracy theories rather than facts. What makes a conspiracy theory so attractive?

2. Have a look at the photo and the comic strip below. With reference to the definition of a conspiracy theory given in the introduction, **point out** which group or organization is being accused of having plotted the 9/11 attacks. Then come up with a suitable caption for each visual.

3. **Comment** on the two different ideas regarding who was actually responsible for 9/11. Take into consideration who might benefit from spreading such a theory.

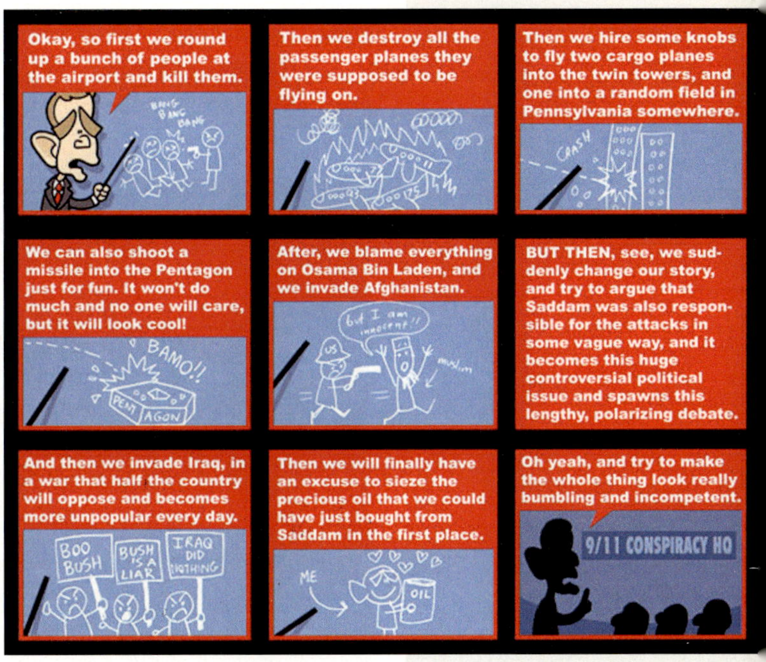

ZOOM IN: Vocabulary

knob *Slang für Idiot* • **to spawn** *erzeugen* • **to sieze (to seize)** *an sich reißen* • **bumbling** *stümperhaft*

M 13 Re: Covers

Art Spiegelman

Art Spiegelman is a Swedish-born American comic artist. He worked for The *New Yorker* for ten years, but resigned shortly after the 9/11 attacks, which he experienced first-hand, living in New York. The cover which he designed for *The New Yorker* issue of 24 September 2001 was widely acclaimed throughout the world. He used it for his graphic novel *In the Shadow of No Towers* which was released in 2004 and deals with his personal traumatic experience and the after-effects of 9/11. In the given text *Re: Covers*, Spiegelman explains how the idea for this cover came into being and what he wanted to express with it.

1. Spiegelman's graphic novel is called *In the Shadow of No Towers*. Have a look at the cover and state in how far the title is reflected by it. Collect suitable adjectives that describe the atmosphere captured here.
2. **Point out** the process of the making of the cover, according to Spiegelman.
3. **Illustrate** how Spiegelman makes use of imagery in order to illustrate his 9/11 trauma.
4. Against the backdrop of lines 31 – 35, **explain** the title of this text.

Cover of Spiegelman's *In the Shadow of No Towers*

ZOOM IN: Vocabulary

- **Umriss** silhouette
- **düster** gloomy
- **hervorstehend** prominent

What is the half-life of memory? My September 11th is finally dimming down to a shadow of itself, to a few compulsively* retold anecdotes and a vivid image or two. As a citizen of Lower Soho, on the outskirts of Ground Zero, I had a ringside seat* to the calamity*, and so my perspective has been slower to shift back to narcotized normalcy than some. If it wasn't for a tremulous* inner voice, singing off-key* along with "my" government's self-

compulsive impossible to control
ringside seat front row seat with an unobstructed view of an event
calamity catastrophe
tremulous unsteady
off-key music or singing that does not sound good because the notes are slightly wrong

serving reminders to Stay Afraid, I might be able to reduce my memory of the vaporized* towers down to size, to little more than last season's most compelling media event. Everyone around the world with access to a television set saw the cataclysmic* destruction of those towers, saw it in constant replay, burning – and burning itself into our collective retina*. What slowed down my own amnesiac responses is simply that I first experienced those events unmediated by television. [...]
Whenever I walked north in the hours and days that followed, I turned back – as if toward Mecca – to see if my buildings were still missing. Not especially well-equipped to help in the search for survivors, I applied myself to searching for an image of the disaster. Despite what felt like the irrelevancy of the task, it gave me a way to fend off* the trauma and focus on something. I wanted to find the awful (and awe*-filled) image of all that disappeared that morning.
I tried to juxtapose* the deadly blackness of the event with the wondrous crystalline blue sky that underscored* the surrealism of that bleak* day. I sketched the towers, shrouded* in black as if by a Christo* in mourning. They floated against a tranquil* Magritte* sky above a Lower Manhattan cityscape. But Surrealism was inadequate to that moment, and the vividness of the color seemed to obscenely mock the blackness at the heart of the picture. I scanned the sketch into my computer, and gradually desaturated* and darkened the color of the sky and cityscape until my screen was virtually black. Only when my picture all but disappeared did it accurately reflect the painful new emptiness I and many others needed to see. [...]
When [my wife] saw the phantom towers on my screen she knew well before I did that I'd found the New Yorker's cover. My work ethic kept insisting that I still needed to render all the buildings that surrounded the World Trade Center, but ultimately, anything other than the most minimal gesture seemed to be an insult to that somber* moment. [...]
The afterimage of the towers lingers*, insisting on its presence through the blackness. But now, in the months of "new normalcy" that have followed, the rescue and salvage* operation that continues near my front stoop* has allowed me the luxury of trying to rescue and salvage my first image. I've "sandblasted" and scrubbed my first sketch and now, with some distance, that blue sky [...] seems at least a little more possible.

Art Spiegelman, "Re: Covers", in: Ulrich Baer (ed.), *110 Stories. New York writes after September 11*, New York University Press, New York/London 2002, pp. 284 – 286

to vaporize to atomize
cataclysmic changing a situation in a sudden and violent way
retina part of the eyes that transforms light signals into images
to fend off to defend yourself against an attack
awe a feeling of great respect, often combined with fear
to juxtapose to place sth. together so that people can see differences
to underscore to emphasize
bleak unpleasant
to shroud to cover sth./to wrap a dead body in a piece of cloth
Christo artist (*1935) famous for wrapping famous buildings
tranquil quiet
Magritte Belgian surrealist artist (1898 – 1967)
to desaturate to remove the colour of a picture
sombre (BrE) serious, or sad
to linger to stay longer than necessary
salvage the action of saving property from being destroyed
stoop (AmE) a raised area outside the front door of a house

5. Have a look at this comic strip, also by Art Spiegelman, published on 11 September 2004. **Discuss** in how far it corresponds to the text *Re: Covers*.

This comic strip was published in the *New York Times* on the occasion of the third anniversary of 9/11 in 2004.

M 14 How to Write a Poem After September 11th

Nikki Moustaki

Nikki Moustaki is a prize-winning American poet who lives in New York. Among other works, she published *The Complete Idiot's Guide to Writing Poetry* in 2001.

1. In her poem, Nikki Moustaki outlines the rules for writing poetry after 9/11. In doing so, she makes use of Dos and Don'ts with reference to words and imagery she considers to be acceptable vs. forbidden or inappropriate. Before reading the poem, make a list of those words and images whose meanings have changed in such a way that they should not be used in poetry any more. Give reasons for your choice.
2. **Point out** which words and images are inappropriate now, according to the poet, and compare your results with your initial ideas.
3. **Compare** Moustaki's feelings about 9/11 to the ones expressed by Meena Alexander (cf. **M10 a, M10 b**). Focus on the use of imagery.
4. **Explain** why Moustaki made use of the example of the mayor "in some other City of Commerce and Art" (ll. 21f.).
5. Adhering to the rules given by Moustaki, write your own 9/11 poem.

First: Don't use the word *souls*. Don't use the word *fire*.
You can use the word *tragic* if you end it with a k.
The rules have changed. The word *building* may precede*
The word fall, but only in the context of the buildings falling
Before the fall, the season we didn't have in Manhattan
Because the weather refused, the air refused ...
Don't say the air smelled like smoldering* desks and drywall*
Ground gypsum*, and something terribly organic,
Don't make a metaphor about the smell, because it wasn't
A smell at all, but the air washed with working souls,
Piling bricks, one by one, spreading mortar*.
Don't compare the planes to birds. Please.
Don't call the windows eyes. We know they saw it coming.
We know they didn't blink. Don't say they were sentinels*.
Say: we hated them then we loved them then they were gone.
Say: we miss them. Say: there's a gap. Then, say something
About love. It's always good in a poem to mention love.
Say: if a man walks down stairs, somewhere
Another man is walking up. Say: He sits at his desk
And the other stands. He answers the phone and the other
Ends a call with a kiss. So, on a rainy dusk in some other
City of Commerce and Art, a mayor cuts a ribbon*
With giant silver scissors. Are you writing this down?
Make the executives parade through the concourse*,
Up the elevators, to the top, where the restaurant,
Open now for the first time, sets out a dinner buffet.
Press hard. Remember, you're writing with ashes.

to precede to come before sth. else
to smoulder (BrE) to burn slowly, producing smoke but no flames
drywall *Trockenbauwand*
gypsum *Gips*
mortar *Mörtel*
sentinel a soldier who stands at the entrance to a place and guards it
ribbon Band
concourse *Eingangshalle*

Nikki Moustaki, "How to write a poem after September 11", in: Dennis Loy Johnson/Valerie Merians (eds.), *Poetry after 9/11. An Anthology of New York Poets. With an introduction by Alicia Ostriker*, Melville House, New York 2002, p. 95

M 15 Random Notes – September 11, 2001, 4:00 P.M.

Paul Auster

Paul Auster

Paul Auster (*1947) is a famous American author whose novels often centre around the quest for identity and tend to mix absurd features with existentialism and crime fiction. Paul Auster lives in Brooklyn, New York, where he experienced the 9/11 attacks first-hand.

1. In his notes on 9/11, Auster states that he thought about his friend Philippe Petit all day long. Have a look at the movie poster provided here and read the information on Petit. What comes to your mind upon seeing the picture? Why do you believe Auster thought about Petit on this terrible day?

2. **Describe** how various people were immediately affected by the attacks, according to Auster.

3. **Examine** in how far the train of thought in the given excerpt corresponds to the title *Random Notes*.

4. Pick another text from this sub-chapter. Put yourself in the shoes of the author/speaker/narrator and write a letter to Mr. Auster in which you express in how far you share his feelings about 9/11.

Man on Wire is a 2008 documentary which tells the story of the French high-wire artist Philippe Petit who, in 1974, performed an illegal high-wire walk between the Twin Towers. The title of the documentary derives from the police report that led to the arrest of Petit.

You can watch the trailer here:

Netcode 40650-005

Zoom in: Vocabulary

Gleichgewicht balance • **Höhe** altitude • **Draufgänger** daredevil • **lebensgefährlich** perilous • **sich beweisen** to prove oneself

Our fourteen-year-old daughter started high school today. For the first time in her life, she rode on the subway from Brooklyn to Manhattan – alone.
She will not be coming home tonight. The subways are no longer running in New York, and my wife and I have arranged for her stay with friends on the Upper West Side.
Less than an hour after she passed under the World Trade Center, the twin towers crumbled to the ground.
From the top floor of our house, we can see the smoke filling the sky of the city. The wind is blowing toward Brooklyn, and the smells of fire have settled into every room of the house. A terrible, stinging odor*: flaming plastic, electric wire, building materials.
My wife's sister, who lives in TriBeCa*, just ten or twelve blocks north of what was once the World Trade Center, called to tell us about the screams she heard after the first tower collapsed. Friends of her, who live on John Street, even closer to the site of the catastrophe, were evacuated by the police after the door of their building was blown in by the impact. They walked north through the rubble* and the debris* – which, they told her, contained human body parts.
After watching the news on television all morning, my wife and I went out for a walk in the neighborhood. Many people were wearing handkerchiefs over their faces. Some wore painters' masks. I stopped and talked to a man who cuts my hair, who was standing in front of his empty barber shop with an anguished* look on his face. A few hours earlier, he said, the woman who owns the antique shop next door had been on the phone with her son-in-law who had been trapped in his office on the 107th floor of the World Trade Center. Less than an hour after she spoke to him, the tower collapsed.
All day, as I have watched the horrific images on the television screen and looked at the smoke through the window, I have been thinking about my friend, the high-wire artist Philippe Petit, who walked between the towers of the World Trade Center in August 1974, just after construction of the buildings was completed. A small man dancing on a wire more than a mile off the ground – an act of indelible* beauty.
Today, that same spot has been turned into a place of death. It frightens me to contemplate* how many people have been killed.
We all knew this could happen. We have been talking about the possibility for years, but now that the tragedy has struck, it's far worse than anyone ever imagined. The last foreign attack on American soil occurred in 1812*. We have no precedent* for what has happened today, and the consequences of this assault will no doubt be terrible. More violence, more death, more pain for everyone.
And so the twenty-first century finally begins. [...]

Paul Auster, "Random Notes – September 11, 2001, 4:00 P.M.; Underground", in: Ulrich Baer (ed.), *110 Stories. New York writes after September 11*, New York University Press, New York/London 2002, pp. 34f.

odour (BrE) an unpleasant smell
TriBeCa "Triangle below Canal Street", a neighbourhood in Lower Manhattan, New York

rubble broken pieces of buildings that have been destroyed
debris the broken pieces that are left when sth. has been destroyed

anguished suffering great physical or emotional pain

indelible permanent

to contemplate to think very carefully about sth. for a long time

1812 reference to the Battle of Baltimore between American and British forces
precedent ['presɪdənt] an action or event in the past that is used as an example or reason for a present action or event

5. "And so the twenty-first century finally begins." (l. 35)
What do you know about the American "retaliation"? Brainstorm in class on measures taken by the Americans in order to "hunt down those who did it!" (George W. Bush)

The Aftermath of 9/11: "Hunting Down Those Who Did It?"

M1 The Clash of Civilizations

Samuel P. Huntington

The American political scientist and Harvard professor Samuel P. Huntington (1927 – 2008) was famous for his 1996 book *The Clash of Civilizations and the Remaking of the World Order*. The text below is an excerpt from an interview he gave to *Islamica Magazine*, which was reprinted by the political journal *New Perspectives Quarterly* (NPQ).

1. A "clash of civilisation" implies that two or more cultures differ in their perception of values. Which aspects do you expect Huntington to bring forward when it comes to the West and Islam and how does he do this? Take into account the cartoon on the right.
2. **Present** the "Clash of Civilizations"-thesis.
3. **Illustrate** how Huntington explains the "failure of democracy to emerge in much of the Muslim world" (ll. 40f.)
4. Write a letter to the editor of *Islamica Magazine* in which you give your personal opinion on whether you agree with Huntington's thesis or not. Prove your points with the help of examples of your own experience when it comes to different cultures living together.

NPQ Your theory on the clash of civilizations argues that global politics today result from deep-seated conflicts between different cultures and religions. This thesis gained momentum* as a result of Sept. 11, and now the war against terrorism is often defined in terms of the West against Islam as a fundamental clash. Do you feel that your thesis has been used or misused since 9/11? Would you moderate* this view in any way?

Samuel Huntington My view is that relations between countries in the coming decades are most likely to reflect their cultural commitments, their cultural ties and antagonism* with other countries rather than other factors. [...] My argument remains that cultural identities, antagonisms and affiliations* will not only play a role, but play a major role in relations between states.

NPQ You have written: "For 45 years, the Iron Curtain* was the central dividing line in Europe. That line has moved several hundred miles east. It is now the line separating the peoples of Western Christianity, on the one hand, from Muslim and Orthodox peoples on the other." Doesn't making such a dichotomous* distinction between the West and Islam imply there is a uniformity within those two categories? Doesn't it ignore the reality that Islamic communities exist within the Western world?

Huntington That implication is totally wrong. I don't suggest that the West is uniform. Obviously there are divisions within the West and divisions within Islam. There are different sects, different communities, different countries. So neither Islam nor the West is homogenous at all. I don't think it is all that useful to think in terms of two solid blocs.

momentum strength or force

to moderate to make sth. less extreme

antagonism strong feeling of disliking sb.

affiliation connection with an organization

Iron Curtain metaphor used by British PM Churchill in 1946 to describe the division of the Cold War world

dichotomous [daɪˈkɒtəməs] a difference between two opposing ideas

commonality sth. you have in common

reconciliation the process of making it possible for two different ideas, facts, etc. to exist together without being opposed to each other

convergence common denominator, similarity

But there is still commonality* within. People everywhere talk about Islam and the West. Presumably that has some relationship to reality and has some meaning. Of course, the core of that reality is differences in religion.

NPQ Is there any reconciliation* or point of convergence* between the two sides of this new "Iron Curtain"?

Huntington As I've said, both sides have divisions. Western countries collaborate with Muslim countries and vice versa. It's a mistake, let me just repeat, to think in terms of two homogenous sides starkly confronting each other. Global politics remains extremely complex and countries have different interests, which will also lead them to make what might seem rather bizarre friends and allies. The United States has cooperated and still is cooperating with various military dictatorships around the world. Obviously we would prefer to see them democratized, but we are doing it because we have national interests, whether it's working with Pakistan or Afghanistan or whomever. [...]

NPQ You've written, "Islamic culture explains, in large part, the failure of democracy to emerge in much of the Muslim world." Yet large parts of the Muslim world have democracy – Indonesia, Mali, Senegal and even India, with its large population of Muslims. What is the connection, or lack of it?

Huntington I don't know what the answer to that question is because I'm not an expert on Islam, but it is striking the relative slowness with which Muslim countries, particularly Arab countries, have moved toward democracy. Their cultural heritage and their ideologies may be in part responsible. The colonial experience they all went through may be a factor in the fight against Western domination, British, French or whatever. Many of these countries were, until recently, largely rural societies with landowning governing elites. I think they are certainly moving toward urbanization and much more pluralistic political systems. In almost every Muslim country, that is occurring. Obviously, they are increasing their involvement with non-Muslim societies. One key aspect that will influence democratization, of course, is the migration of Muslims into Europe. [...]

NPQ How do you think that fundamentalism – the radical idea that one's own identity is superior to all others – influences global politics today? Do you think there is a particular radicalism that is only associated with Islam, or do you think it exists in all faiths?

Huntington I think fundamentalism is what you said: this radical attitude toward one's own identity and civilization as compared to other people's identities and cultures. Fundamentalist tendencies and movements have existed in all societies and civilizations. Certainly here in the US, we've had fundamentalist movements that have taken very critical and hostile attitudes toward immigration and the assimilation of immigrants into our society and culture. So these tendencies are fairly universal. The problem is when these fundamentalist attitudes get out of hand and become the dominant factor in a society, which can only lead to the oppression of minorities or even to war with neighboring societies with differing cultures. That's why it's important to try to keep these tendencies toward extremism under control. [...]

Amina R. Chaudary, "The Clash of Civilizations Revisited", in: *New Perspectives Quarterly*, vol. 24 #1, winter 2007, www.digitalnpq.org [06.09.2012]

M2 God, Love and the Terrorists

Jane Shaw

The following article was published in the British newspaper *The Guardian* on 22 September 2001 and deals with how religious fanaticism contributes to terrorism.

1. After having read the headline of the newspaper article, make an educated guess on how these three words are connected with each other.

2. Briefly **state** the two opinions about the connection of religion and terrorism as presented in the article and compare them with your hypothesis.

3. **Explain** Shaw's arguments as to how religion and terrorism are connected.

Can religion be held responsible for atrocities* of the sort that occurred in New York and Washington? In last Saturday's *Guardian*, Richard Dawkins, Oxford University's professor for the public understanding of science, fellow of my college and an atheist, blamed religion for the terrorist attacks. He ended with this inflammatory* comment: "To fill a world with religion, or religions, of the Abrahamic kind, is like littering the streets with loaded guns. Do not be surprised if they are used."

There is some truth in the overall argument that religion can be used to cause harm. The belief that they will be rewarded in heaven fuels many a suicide bomber, as do images of a vengeful, intolerant God who loves only select bands of human beings rather than all humanity. Such beliefs are not only found in extreme Islam. The language of retribution* and a judgmental God is there in some Hebrew and Christian scriptures, and we cannot deny that Christianity has often perpetuated* violence.

But Dawkins has missed the main point that all belief systems, all value systems, can be used for evil or good – including science. Where would last week's terrorists have been without the scientific technology that makes aeroplanes? A fundamental truth about human beings is that we have the capacity to turn good to evil purpose.

It is irresponsible to blame, in a blanket way, "religion" or "science" or "Islam" or "Christianity", or any other large cultural movement for such atrocities. We need to understand the context in which a belief system has been nurtured – or perverted – and, finally, put into practice.

If indeed, the terrorist attacks on the United States were attacks on the Christian west, as is generally thought, that too is a dangerous stereotype. Since its 1965 Immigration Act*, the religious landscape of America has been radically altered*. It has gone from "a Christian country" to becoming the most religiously diverse nation in the world, with Islam the fastest growing religion. There are more Muslims in the US than Presbyterians, Episcopalians or Jews.

In Britain, too, we acknowledge the diversity of cultures and religions in which we live, also largely a result of postwar immigration patterns. And yet, almost everywhere, we see the use of the stereotype for each other, and expressions of intolerance and hatred.

There is a verse in the Koran, "Do you not know, O people, that I have made you into tribes and nations that you may know each other." And yet, we mostly do not know each other. We still have that work to do. "Getting to know each other," is a great challenge.

Yasmin Alibhai-Brown, the British Muslim writer, has urged us, as a nation, to get to know each other: "Somehow we need to break away from the foolish idea that we are all forever fated to remain disconnected, to shout across ravines* and canyons at one another or gripe* amongst ourselves about those on the other side."

atrocity brutality, barbarity

inflammatory provocative

retribution payback for another's action

to perpetuate to keep sth. going

Richard Dawkins

Immigration Act Act which regulated immigration on the basis of the immigrants' skills rather than on a specific quota

to alter to change

ravine gap in earth's surface

to gripe to complain

abundant plentiful, large in number

incarnate in bodily form

This is a practical way forward, but what religion provides, at its best, is an important emotional and spiritual component to all of this practice: love. Those of us who are Christians must always ensure that we keep the God of love at the forefront of our religious practice. The two great commandments are "Love thy God" and "Love thy neighbour as thyself". We have seen abundant* examples of these commandments at work in the aftermath of last week's atrocity. At the heart of Christianity is the message that God loves all of us individually, and – as the incarnate* God, Christ, came to earth to show – shares our human love and suffering.
God's love also tells us something about the nature of human love at its best. That love is demonstrated in the actions of neighbour helping neighbour, stranger helping stranger – today, yesterday, tomorrow, and, in the weeks and months to come, in New York. Just as God's love is demonstrated to each one of us individually, so our capacity to love comes alive as we demonstrate our love for each other, in acts of compassion, empathy and self-giving. And the more we do that, the more we find ourselves having the capacity to love. The more we love, the better we act at it; in this, human beings are truly made in the image and likeness of God.
These terrible events have evoked grief, compassion, anger, frustration. But if the religion we have, and we say we believe in, means anything to us, then it must evoke the strongest desire to act on, and demonstrate, God's love in all that we do.

Jane Shaw, "God, Love and the Terrorists", www.guardian.co.uk, 22.09.2001 [06.09.2012]

Netcode 40650-006

4. Visit the website which contains the article by Richard Dawkins referred to in the text. For further information have a look at the Wikipedia article about Dawkins, especially the paragraph *Advocacy of atheism*. Put Richard Dawkins on the Hot Seat!

M3 "Yes, This Is About Islam"

Salman Rushdie

In this *New York Times* article from 2 November 2001, Salman Rushdie comments on the connection between the 9/11 attacks and Islam.

ZOOM IN: People

Salman Rushdie

The Indian-British essayist and novelist Sir Ahmad Salman Rushdie was born in Bombay, India, on 19 June 1947. He comes from an educated family, his father being a businessman and his mother a teacher. Rushdie studied history at the University of Cambridge.
Rushdie became famous after his fourth novel *The Satanic Verses* aroused a great deal of controversy in Muslim countries. As a result, he was confronted with a fatwa (in this case, a death sentence) against him by the Supreme Leader of Iran, Ayatollah Ruhollah Khomeini, in 1989, which forced him to live under police protection for several years.

Salman Rushdie

1. After reading the article, **explain** its title.

2. **Analyse** how Rushdie characterizes present-day Islamic tendencies. Which attitude does he express and how is this conveyed?

3. **Compare** Huntington's and Rushdie's approaches in regards to the relationship between the Western world and Islam.

4. **Discuss** Rushdie's proposals to attempt to reconcile Islam with modernity.

"This isn't about Islam." The world's leaders have been repeating this mantra for weeks, partly in the virtuous hope of deterring* reprisal attacks on innocent Muslims living in the West, partly because if the United States is to maintain its coalition against terror it can't afford to suggest that Islam and terrorism are in any way related. The trouble with this necessary disclaimer* is that it isn't true. If this isn't about Islam, why the worldwide Muslim demonstrations in support of Osama bin Laden and Al Qaeda? Why did those 10,000 men armed with swords and axes mass on the Pakistan-Afghanistan frontier, answering some mullahs call to jihad? Why are the war's first British casualties* three Muslim men who died fighting on the Taliban side? [...]

Of course this is "about Islam." The question is, what exactly does that mean? After all, most religious belief isn't very theological. Most Muslims are not profound Koranic analysts. For a vast number of "believing" Muslim men, "Islam" stands, in a jumbled, half-examined way, not only for the fear of God, the fear more than the love, one suspects, but also for a cluster of customs, opinions and prejudices that include their dietary practices; the sequestration* or near-sequestration of "their" women; the sermons* delivered by their mullahs of choice; a loathing* of modern society in general, riddled as it is with music, godlessness and sex; and a more particularized loathing (and fear) of the prospect that their own immediate surroundings could be taken over – "Westoxicated" – by the liberal Western-style way of life.

Highly motivated organizations of Muslim men (oh, for the voices of Muslim women to be heard!) have been engaged over the last 30 years or so in growing radical political movements out of this mulch* of "belief." These Islamists – we must get used to this word, "Islamists," meaning those who are engaged upon such political projects, and learn to distinguish it from the more general and politically neutral "Muslim" – include the Muslim Brotherhood in Egypt, the blood-soaked combatants of the Islamic Salvation Front and Armed Islamic Group in Algeria, the Shiite revolutionaries of Iran, and the Taliban. Poverty is their great helper, and the fruit of their efforts is paranoia. This paranoid Islam, which blames outsiders, "infidels," for all the ills of Muslim societies, and whose proposed remedy is the closing of those societies to the rival project of modernity, is presently the fastest growing version of Islam in the world.

This is not wholly to go along with Samuel Huntington's thesis about the clash of civilizations, for the simple reason that the Islamists' project is turned not only against the West and "the Jews", but also against their fellow Islamists. Whatever the public rhetoric, there's little love lost between the Taliban and Iranian regimes. Dissensions between Muslim nations run at least as deep, if not deeper, than those nations' resentment of the West. Nevertheless, it would be absurd to deny that this self-exculpatory*, paranoiac Islam is an ideology with widespread appeal.

Twenty years ago, when I was writing a novel about power struggles in a fictionalized Pakistan, it was already de rigueur* in the Muslim world to blame all its troubles on the West and, in particular, the United States. [...] But I wanted then to ask a question that is no less important now: Suppose we say that the ills of our societies are not primarily

to deter [dɪ'tɛːr] to make sb. decide not to do sth.

disclaimer a written statement in which a company or person says they do not take responsibility for sth. bad

casualty a person who is killed or injured in war or in an incident

sequestration deprivation

sermon speech made by a priest or another religious person during a religious ceremony

to loathe to hate

mulch decaying leaves or other plant material used for improving the soil

to exculpate to prove that sb. is not guilty of a crime

de rigueur [rɪ'gɜː] necessary in order to be accepted

America's fault, that we are to blame for our own failings? How would we understand them then? Might we not, by accepting our own responsibility for our problems, begin to learn to solve them for ourselves?

Many Muslims, as well as secularist* analysts with roots in the Muslim world, are beginning to ask such questions now. In recent weeks Muslim voices have everywhere been raised against the obscurantist* hijacking of their religion. [...] An Iraqi writer quotes an earlier Iraqi satirist: "The disease that is in us, is from us." A British Muslim writes, "Islam has become its own enemy." A Lebanese friend, returning from Beirut, tells me that in the aftermath of the attacks on Sept. 11, public criticism of Islamism has become much more outspoken. Many commentators have spoken of the need for a Reformation in the Muslim world. [...] If Islam is to be reconciled with modernity, these voices must be encouraged until they swell into a roar. Many of them speak of another Islam, their personal, private faith.

The restoration of religion to the sphere of the personal, its depoliticization, is the nettle* that all Muslim societies must grasp in order to become modern. The only aspect of modernity interesting to the terrorists is technology, which they see as a weapon that can be turned on its makers. If terrorism is to be defeated, the world of Islam must take on board the secularist-humanist principles on which the modern is based, and without which Muslim countries' freedom will remain a distant dream.

Salman Rushdie, "Yes, This Is about Islam", www.nytimes.com, 02.11.2001 [06.09.2012]

secularist not religious

obscurantism deliberately making things more confusing so that people don't know the truth

to grasp the nettle (BrE) to deal with a difficult situation firmly and without hesitating

M 4 Despite Protests, Mosque Plan Near 9/11 Site Wins Key Vote

Ray Sanchez

In early 2010, the idea to build an Islamic cultural centre near Ground Zero was proposed. However, voices against such a plan became loud. In this article from *abcnews.go.com* from 26 May 2010, journalist Ray Sanchez explains the issue.

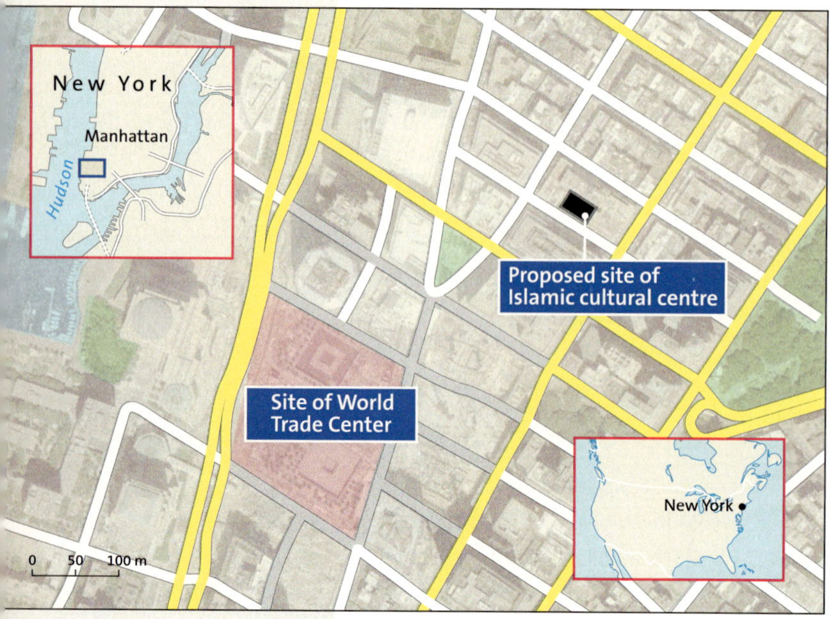

1. Before reading the article, anticipate which arguments might be brought forward by the opponents of the Islamic cultural centre. Compare your thoughts with a partner.

2. **Describe** the arguments presented in the article and compare them with your answers from Task 1.

3. Compare the pro- and counter-arguments presented in the article and rank them according to your personal opinion (1 = most convincing, 4 = least convincing). Then talk to a partner and agree on the most and least convincing argument.

Opponents called it an "insult," "demeaning*" and a "house of evil", but the angry protests did not stop an advisory board* from approving plans to build a mosque and Islamic center two blocks from the site of the 9/11 attacks on the World Trade Center.

In a heated, four hour meeting Tuesday night, Community Board 1, which represents the area of lower Manhattan that includes Ground Zero, voted 29-1 in favor of the proposal. There were 10 abstentions*. At the raucous* meeting, some relatives carried signs with the faces of 9/11 victims, reflecting still-raw emotions nearly a decade after the terrorist attacks.

"This is an insult", said one of the more than 150 people at the meeting. "This is demeaning. This is humiliating that you would build a shrine to the very ideology that inspired the attacks on 9/11."

Angrily pointing a finger at board members, another protester said: "This house of evil will be the birthplace of the next terrorist event."

But Community Board 1 member Rob Townley called the plan a "seed of peace," a message repeated by mosque supporters throughout the night.

"We believe that this is a significant step in the Muslim community to counteract the hate and fanaticism in the minority of the community," he said.

Imam Feisal Abdul Rauf, the man behind the mosque proposal, said he understood the pain and outrage, especially since Muslims also died in the attacks.

"We have condemned the actions of 9/11," Abdul Rauf said. "We have condemned terrorism."

Still, plans to build a mosque and Islamic community center could be thwarted* by the New York City's Landmarks Commission, which will hold a hearing on the matter in the early summer.

The proposal to build an Islamic center and mosque just blocks from the city's most hallowed* ground has divided survivors of the nearly 3,000 people who perished on Sept. 11, 2001, with many families vehemently opposed to the plan.

Many have complained that it would be insensitive to have a huge mosque two blocks from the site that became the burial ground for victims of the 9/11 terror attack by Muslim militants of Al Qaeda. [...]

Noah Pfefferblit, Community Board 1's district manager, said the board voted on a resolution in favor of the plan's community center without taking a position on the mosque.

"Most of the resolutions are approved but this is an unusual one because it's been very controversial," he said. "Our members would not be comfortable recommending or not recommending a house of worship."

The mosque is only one component of the Islamic center complex, which also includes a swimming pool, performance space and a basketball court. The center is the brainchild* of Abdul Rauf, a New York imam, and Daisy Khan, executive director of the American Society for Muslim Advancement.

The couple hopes to raise the estimated $100 million to raze* the building at 45 Park Place to make room for the multi-story glass-and-steel structure two blocks from ground zero.

The Islamic center would be known as Cordoba House and include a mosque for up to 1,500 worshippers on Fridays. Some 500 people already use the site of the old Burlington Coat Factory for Friday prayers.

Ray Sanchez, "Despite Protests, Mosque Plan Near 9/11 Site Wins Key Vote", http://abcnews.go.com, 26.05.2010 [06.09.2012]

to demean to humiliate
advisory board planning board
abstention *Enthaltung*
raucous ['rɔːkəs] noisy, rough
to thwart to stop, to hinder
hallowed respected and important
brainchild invention
to raze to remove

4. Stage a talk show between supporters and opponents of the planned mosque. Here are some suggestions for possible participants: a conservative politician, Daisy Khan, member of the advisory board, a wife whose husband died in the WTC. Feel free to come up with different participants!

M5 Crash

Paul Haggis

The drama film *Crash* (German title *L.A. Crash*) from 2004, directed by Paul Haggis, deals with social and racial tensions in Los Angeles, California. In various episodes, it tells the story of different characters who are dealing with racism. During the film it becomes obvious that the characters are not only victims of racism, but are also racists themselves. The film won three Oscars in 2005.

In this episode, Farhad, a Persian shop owner, enters a gun store together with his daughter Dorri, in order to buy a revolver. During the conversation with the shop owner, Farhad is confronted with racist comments.

Scene from the film

1. Briefly **summarise** what the conversation is about.
2. Obviously, the salesman Dirk is prejudiced against Farhad, a Muslim who wants to buy a gun. **Illustrate** when and why both Farhad and Dirk talk at cross-purposes.
3. After Dorri leaves the gun shop, she meets Farhad in the car. Farhad is still upset about the conversation he had with the shop owner. Write Dorri and Farhad's dialogue.

The handgun slides onto the counter. The hand belongs to DIRK, *the impatient salesman.*
DIRK: You get one free box of ammunition, what kind you want?
[...]
FARHAD, *Iranian, 50s, looks at the handgun and turns to his daughter* DORRI, *25, who wears a blue suit and a bad mood.*
FARHAD *(in Farsi)*: What did he say "ammunition"?
DORRI *(in Farsi)*: He asked what kind of bullets you want.
FARHAD *(in Farsi)*: The kind that fit the gun!
DORRI *(in Farsi)*: There's more than one type.
FARHAD *(in Farsi)*: How do I know? I don't know anything about bullets.
DORRI *(in Farsi)*: Which is a really good reason not to be buying a gun.
FARHAD *(in Farsi)*: You don't use that tone of voice with me.
DIRK: Yo, Osama, plan the Jihad on your own time; what do you want?
FARHAD *(in Farsi)*: What is he saying about Jihad? *(to* DIRK *in English)* Are you making insults at me?
DIRK: Am I making insults at you??? That's the closest you get to English?
FARHAD: I am American citizen –!
DIRK: – Oh God.
FARHAD: – I have rights like you! I have right to buy gun!
Dirk pulls the gun back to his side of the counter.
DIRK: Not from my store, you don't.

DIRK *nods towards the Security Guard, who heads his way.* DORRI *sees him coming.*

DORRI: Go wait in the car, Dad.

FARHAD *(to* DIRK*)*: You are ignorant man!

DIRK: Yeah, I'm ignorant, you're liberating my country and I'm flying 747s into your mud huts and incinerating* your friends. Get the fuck out of my store.

SEC. GUARD *(taking his arm)*: Let's go.

FARHAD: You don't touch! This man cheats me!

DORRI *(to* FARHAD*)*: Do you want to get arrested? Go wait in the car, Dad!

FARHAD *storms out, the security guard following.* DORRI *looks the salesman dead in the eye.*

DORRI *(cont'd)*: You can give me the gun or give me the money back, and I'm really hoping for the money.

DIRK *looks* DORRI *up and down, gives her a lecherous* smile and slides, the gun back across the counter*

Paul Haggis & Bobby Moresco, *Crash* (Screenplay), 2004, www.awesomefilm.com [06.09.2012]

to incinerate to reduce to ashes

lecherous ['letʃərəs] lustful

4. This photograph by Ridz Design was taken for the *Illume Magazine* 9/11 anniversary issue on Muslims in the US. It deals with Islamophobia and shows the duality of people who are both whole-heartedly Muslim as well as American.
Relate the photograph to the scene presented above: In how far does it reflect Farhad's experiences in the gun shop? Talk to your partner about your ideas and compare them.

M 6 The USA Patriot Act

On 25 October 2001, Congress passed the so-called USA Patriot Act (Uniting and Strengthening America by Providing Appropriate Tools Required to Intercept and Obstruct Terrorism Act of 2001) as an immediate reaction to the 9/11 attacks.

1. Since the Patriot Act was passed in order to make investigations for federal institutions easier, it also limited certain basic rights. Which basic rights would you limit if you were a member of the Department of Justice and in charge of developing the Patriot Act?

2. **Describe** the differences in dealing with crimes and terrorism-related events before the Patriot Act and after. What are the differences and in how far does the Patriot Act facilitate investigations?

3. Lynn Woosley, the representative of California, wrote "that Congress would have blood on its hands if there was another terrorist attack while we deliberated [argued]." **Comment** on this statement.

law enforcement police

fraud [frɔːd] trickery, deception
wiretap device for listening without permission

sophisticated experienced
to evade to escape
to rove to move
to racketeer to commit crimes
to thwart to stop

subpoena [səb'piːnə] court order

to be at sb.'s disposal to be accessible for sb.

Allows law enforcement* to use surveillance against more crimes of terror.
Before the Patriot Act, courts could permit law enforcement to conduct electronic surveillance to investigate many ordinary, non-terrorism crimes, such as drug crimes, mail fraud*, and passport fraud. Agents also could obtain wiretaps* to investigate some, but not all, of the crimes that terrorists often commit. The Act enabled investigators to gather information when looking into the full range of terrorism-related crimes, including: chemical-weapons offenses, the use of weapons of mass destruction, killing Americans abroad, and terrorism financing.

Allows federal agents to follow sophisticated* terrorists trained to evade* detection.
For years, law enforcement has been able to use "roving* wiretaps" to investigate ordinary crimes, including drug offenses and racketeering*. A roving wiretap can be authorized by a federal judge to apply to a particular suspect, rather than a particular phone or communications device. Because international terrorists are sophisticated and trained to thwart* surveillance by rapidly changing locations and communication devices such as cell phones, the Act authorized agents to seek court permission to use the same techniques in national security investigations to track terrorists. [...]

Allows federal agents to ask a court for an order to obtain business records in national security terrorism cases.
Examining business records often provides the key that investigators are looking for to solve a wide range of crimes. Investigators might seek select records from hardware stores or chemical plants, for example, to find out who bought materials to make a bomb, or bank records to see who's sending money to terrorists. Law enforcement authorities have always been able to obtain business records in criminal cases through grand jury subpoenas*, and continue to do so in national security cases where appropriate. [...] In national security cases where use of the grand jury process was not appropriate, investigators previously had limited tools at their disposal* to obtain certain business records. Under the Patriot Act, the government can now ask a federal court (the Foreign Intelligence Surveillance Court), if needed to aid an investigation, to order production of the same type of records available through grand jury subpoenas. [...]

The Patriot Act increased the penalties for those who commit terrorist crimes. Americans are threatened as much by the terrorist who pays for a bomb as by the one who pushes the button. That's why the Patriot Act imposed tough new penalties on those who commit and support terrorist operations, both at home and abroad. In particular, the Act:

Prohibits the harboring* of terrorists. The Act created a new offense that prohibits knowingly harboring persons who have committed or are about to commit a variety of terrorist offenses, such as: destruction of aircraft; use of nuclear, chemical, or biological weapons; use of weapons of mass destruction; bombing of government property; sabotage of nuclear facilities; and aircraft piracy.

Enhanced the inadequate maximum penalties for various crimes likely to be committed by terrorists: including arson*, destruction of energy facilities, material support to terrorists and terrorist organizations, and destruction of national-defense materials. [...]

Department of Justice (ed.), "The USA PATRIOT Act: Preserving Life and Liberty", 2001, www.justice.gov [06.09.2012]

to harbor (AmE) to hide, to protect

arson intentional burning

4. The cartoon on p. 50 depicts Patrick Henry, a fighter for American independence back in 1775, and former US president George W. Bush. Go to the website indicated on the right and find out more about Patrick Henry and his role during the American Revolution. Prepare a presentation in which you explain the connection made by the cartoonist concerning the role of liberty.

Netcode 40650-007

5. Not only the United States of America was deeply concerned about improving its legislation. The 9/11 attacks also had a huge impact on other countries' legislation, including Germany's. Search the Internet for information about how Germany tightened its measures concerning "those who did it" or possible suspects.

M7 State of the Union Address, 2002

George W. Bush

This State of the Union address from 29 January 2002 was the first one given after the 9/11 attacks. It became famous due to its rather aggressive rhetoric.

1. **Point out** what is meant by the "axis of evil", how Bush sees the relationship between Islam and Christianity and, consequently, what America's task is.
2. **Analyse** how Bush gets his message across with regard to rhetoric.
3. **Assess** the impact a speech like this might have on international relations.

Netcode 40650-008

[...] Our cause is just, and it continues. Our discoveries in Afghanistan confirmed our worst fears and showed us the true scope of the task ahead. We have seen the depth of our enemies' hatred in videos where they laugh about the loss of innocent life. [...]

Our second goal is to prevent regimes that sponsor terror from threatening America or our friends and allies with weapons of mass destruction. Some of these regimes have been pretty quiet since September 11, but we know their true nature. North Korea is a regime arming with missiles* and weapons of mass destruction, while starving its citizens. Iran aggressively pursues these weapons and exports terror, while an unelected few repress the Iranian people's hope for freedom. Iraq continues to flaunt* its hostility toward America and to support terror. The Iraqi regime has plotted to develop anthrax and nerve

missile ['mɪsaɪl] explosive weapon

to flaunt to show proudly

indifference lack of interest

to splinter to fall apart

resolve determination

awe great respect and admiration

to aspire to want

servitude the state of being a slave

exempt from allowed to ignore sth.

to advocate to support

gas and nuclear weapons for over a decade. This is a regime that has already used poison gas to murder thousands of its own citizens, leaving the bodies of mothers huddled over their dead children. This is a regime that agreed to international inspections then kicked out the inspectors. This is a regime that has something to hide from the civilized world. States like these, and their terrorist allies, constitute an axis of evil, arming to threaten the peace of the world. By seeking weapons of mass destruction, these regimes pose a grave and growing danger. They could provide these arms to terrorists, giving them the means to match their hatred. They could attack our allies or attempt to blackmail the United States. In any of these cases, the price of indifference* would be catastrophic. [...]

During these last few months, I've been humbled and privileged to see the true character of this country in a time of testing. Our enemies believed America was weak and materialistic, that we would splinter* in fear and selfishness. They were as wrong as they are evil. The American people have responded magnificently, with courage and compassion, strength and resolve*. As I have met the heroes, hugged the families and looked into the tired faces of rescuers, I have stood in awe* of the American people. [...]

And we have a great opportunity during this time of war to lead the world toward the values that will bring lasting peace. All fathers and mothers, in all societies, want their children to be educated and live free from poverty and violence. No people on Earth yearn to be oppressed, or aspire* to servitude*, or eagerly await the midnight knock of the secret police. If anyone doubts this, let them look to Afghanistan, where the Islamic "street" greeted the fall of tyranny with song and celebration. Let the skeptics look to Islam's own rich history – with its centuries of learning, and tolerance, and progress.

America will lead by defending liberty and justice because they are right and true and unchanging for all people everywhere. No nation owns these aspirations, and no nation is exempt* from them. We have no intention of imposing our culture – but America will always stand firm for the non-negotiable demands of human dignity: the rule of law ... limits on the power of the state ... respect for women ... private property ... free speech ... equal justice ... and religious tolerance. America will take the side of brave men and women who advocate* these values around the world – including the Islamic world – be-

cause we have a greater objective than eliminating threats and containing resentment. We seek a just and peaceful world beyond the war on terror. [...]
In a single instant, we realized that this will be a decisive decade in the history of liberty – that we have been called to a unique role in human events. Rarely has the world faced a choice more clear or consequential. Our enemies send other people's children on missions of suicide and murder. They embrace tyranny and death as a cause and a creed*. We stand for a different choice – made long ago, on the day of our founding. We affirm it again today. We choose freedom and the dignity of every life. Steadfast* in our purpose, we now press on. We have known freedom's price. We have shown freedom's power. And in this great conflict, my fellow Americans, we will see freedom's victory.
Thank you, thank you all, and may God bless.

creed belief

steadfast constant

"State of the Union Address", www.cnn.com, 29.01.2002 [06.09.2012]

4. The cartoon on p. 52 suggests that, from an American perspective, Iraq, Syria, North Korea, Iran and Cuba belong to the axis of evil. Why is that? Form groups. Each group chooses one country to present in class. Do Internet research in order to find out more details about your country and why, according to Bush it is a so-called "rogue state" [*Schurkenstaat*]. Then present your findings (PowerPoint, poster, etc.).

M 8 Bin Laden

Immortal Technique

Immortal Technique (AKA Felipe Coronel) is an American rapper of Peruvian origin living in New York. He committed several crimes for which he was sent to prison. During his imprisonment, he studied the works of Che Guevara (fighter for Cuban independence) and Malcolm X (a leader of the American Civil Rights Movement) which strongly inspired him. In 2004, he released the song *Bin Laden* together with fellow hip hop artists Mos Def and Eminem.

Immortal Technique

1. Focus on the first verse and **outline** the artist's criticism brought forward here.

2. **Point out** the artist's message in the second verse.

3. **Examine** the choice of words used in this song and how they emphasize its message.

4. Imagine you are a music journalist and have the opportunity to interview Immortal Technique. Come up with at least five questions you would like to ask him about his song. Then find a partner and compare your questions. Agree on the three most interesting ones and together write the interview.

[Mos Def – talking]
Man, you hear this bullshit they be talkin'
Every day, man
It's like these motherfuckers is just like professional liars
You know what I'm sayin? It's wild
Listen

[Hook – Mos Def]
Bin Laden didn't blow up the projects
It was you, nigga
Tell the truth, nigga
(Bush knocked down the towers)
Tell the truth, nigga
(Bush knocked down the towers)
Tell the truth, nigga

Bin Laden didn't blow up the projects
[...]

to pledge allegiance to express loyalty to the USA
leech parasite
to track to follow
to frame sb. *jdm. etw. anhängen*
tryna (sl.) trying to
indictment [ɪn'daɪtmənt] accusation
they their
mansion very large house
to fund to finance
tactician agent

[Verse 1 – Immortal Technique]
I pledge no allegiance*, nigga fuck the president's speeches
I'm baptized by America and covered in leeches*
The dirty water that bleaches your soul and your facial features
Drownin' you in propaganda that they spit through the speakers
And if you speak about the evil that the government does
The Patriot Act'll track* you to the type of your blood
They try to frame* you, and say you was tryna* sell drugs
And throw a federal indictment* on niggaz to show you love
This shit is run by fake Christians, fake politicians
Look at they* mansions*, then look at the conditions you live in
All they talk about is terrorism on television
They tell you to listen, but they don't really tell you they mission
They funded* Al-Qaeda, and now they blame the Muslim religion
Even though Bin Laden was a CIA tactician*
They gave him billions of dollars, and they funded his purpose
Fahrenheit 9/11, that's just scratchin' the surface

[Hook – Mos Def]
Bin Laden didn't blow up the projects
[...]

hood neighbourhood
to clock to beat
mercenary *(adj.)* greedy
contractor business-person
strapped *angeschnallt*
Lee Malvo serial killer who killed ten people in Washington in 2002
sniper rifle Scharfschützengewehr

[Verse 2 – Immortal Technique]
They say the rebels in Iraq still fight for Saddam
But that's bullshit, I'll show you why it's totally wrong
Cuz if another country invaded the hood* tonight
It'd be warfare through Harlem, and Washington Heights
I wouldn't be fightin' for Bush or White America's dream
I'd be fightin' for my people's survival and self-esteem
I wouldn't fight for racist churches from the south, my nigga
I'd be fightin' to keep the occupation out, my nigga
You ever clock* someone who talk shit, or look at you wrong?
Imagine if they shot at you, and was rapin' your moms
And of course Saddam Hussein had chemical weapons
We sold him that shit, after Ronald Reagan's election
Mercenary* contractors* fightin' a new era
Corporate military bankin' off the war on terror
They controllin' the ghetto, with the failed attack
Tryna distract the fact that they engineerin' the crack
So I'm strapped* like Lee Malvo* holdin' a sniper rifle*

These bullets'll touch your kids, and I don't mean like Michael*
Your body be sent to the morgue*, stripped down and recycled
I fire on house niggaz that support you and like you
Cuz innocent people get murdered in the struggle daily
And poor people never get shit and struggle daily
This ain't no alien conspiracy theory, this shit is real
Written on the dollar underneath the Masonic seal*

(I don't rap for dead presidents
I'd rather see the president dead
It's never been said but I set precedents*) – [Eminem]

[Hook – Mos Def]
Bin Laden didn't blow up the projects
[...]

(Shady Records was 80 seconds away from the towers
Some cowards fucked with the wrong building, they meant to hit ours) –
[Eminem]

Immortal Technique, "Bin Laden", Babygrande Records 2005

Michael allusion to the accusation that Michael Jackson molested children
morgue *Leichenhalle*

Masonic seal picture on US one-dollar bill depicting a pyramid with an eye on top

precedent authoritative example

5. Watch the video on *YouTube*.
What kind of video is it? Do you think that this kind of video effectively supports the artist's message? Would you have chosen another type of visualisation? Why (not)? Write a video review.

Netcode 40650-009

M 9 God Bless This Mess

Sheryl Crow

Sheryl Crow (*1961) is an American singer-songwriter and musician who also participated in an MTV 9/11 tribute concert.

1. "God Bless This Mess" is a saying that appears on wall hangings and knick-knacks [= a small cheap object used as decoration] in some American homes. The phrase implies resignation that the constant clutter [the mess created when there are too many things in a place] is a way of life.
from: www.songfacts.com [04.04.2012]
Taking the explanation above into account, make an educated guess on how Sheryl Crow relates the saying "God Bless This Mess" to the after-effects of 9/11. Be as specific as possible in regards to the "things" that cause the "clutter".

2. **Describe** the situation the speaker finds her-/himself in.

3. **Point out** how Sheryl Crow characterises America's situation and what she specifically criticises.

4. Listen to the song and **explain** how the melody and the singer's voice underline its message. Make use of the language support provided.

ZOOM IN: Vocabulary

Talking about songs

The music is ...

- instrumental – rhythmic – powerful – catchy – optimistic – dissonant – melodious – soft – loud – lively – energetic – fast – slow – sad – uplifting – cheerful – monotonous ...

The music ...

- creates a feeling of suspense – danger – happiness – joy – sadness ...

The song has ...

- a pleasant – catchy ... melody.
- a simple rhythm – chorus ...

The mood is ...

- sad – aggressive – calming – angry – excited – relaxing – moving – joyful – optimistic – disturbing – harsh – bitter ...

The singer's voice is ...

- deep – husky – hoarse – high-pitched – soothing

Daddy's in the hallway
Hanging pictures on the wall
And mama's in the kitchen
Making casseroles* for all

casserole food prepared in a deep dish with a lid, used for cooking a mixture of meat, vegetables, etc. in the oven

My brother came home yesterday
From somewhere far away
He doesn't look like I remember
He just stares off into space
He must've seen some awful things
He just can't seem to say

Chorus
Oh, God bless this mess
God bless this mess
God bless this mess

Sheryl Crow

I got a job in town
Selling insurance on the phone
With Robert and Teresa
And two con men* from back home
But everyone I call up doesn't have the time to chat
Everybody is so busy doing this and doing that
But something has gone missing
And it makes me kind of sad

con man (coll.) trickster

Chorus

I heard about the day
That two skyscrapers came down
Firemen, policemen
People came from all around
The smoke covered the city
And the body count did rise

And the president spoke words of comfort
With tears in his eyes
Then he led us as a nation
Into a war based on lies

Chorus

Sheryl Crow, "God Bless this Mess", Album: "Detours", A&M Records 2008, Text: Sheryl Suzanne Crow, © First State Media Group Ltd., Chrysalis Music Holdings GmbH, Berlin

5. You have already studied President Bush's address delivered immediately after the 9/11 attacks, which Sheryl Crow also refers to in lines 30/31.
Put yourself in the shoes of either the speaker of this song or President Bush and prepare a five-minute talk in which you justify your view on the Iraq War. Think of at least three rhetorical devices to employ in order to make your talk as convincing as possible. Take notes of key words only so that you can speak freely. Do not forget to establish eye contact with your audience.

The Legacy of 9/11: Chapter or Footnote?

M1 The New Ground Zero

The term Ground Zero originates from the American nuclear bombing of Japan in 1945. In general, it describes the point on the ground directly beneath a detonation. However, today the term is associated with the site of the 9/11 attacks in New York City, where the World Trade Center was located.
Soon after the attacks, then-President Bush vowed to rebuild the Center in order to turn it into a symbol of American resolve and to show that the US is not intimidated by terrorist attacks. The centrepiece is going to be a building called One World Trade Center, but there will be further office buildings named World Trade Center as well, to be distinguished by their numbers. In the centre of the site there will be the World Trade Center Memorial, containing a museum as well as a memorial site.

1. With the help of the pictures below, **explain** how the architectural design is supposed to show "American resolve".

2. **Discuss** whether this architectural design was the best way to commemorate 9/11. Think of alternatives as well.

The new Ground Zero

Zoom in: Vocabulary

Wolkenkratzer skyscraper • **widerspiegeln** to reflect • **glänzen** to shine • **etw. überragen** to tower over sth. • **von weitem** from afar • **Spitze** tip

M 2 A New Beginning

Barack Obama

"A New Beginning" is the title of a speech which Barack Obama delivered at Cairo University in Egypt in 2009. The programmatic title already indicates that Obama sought to find this "new beginning" in the relations between the US and the Muslim world.

ZOOM IN: People

Barack Obama

Barack Obama

Barack Obama is the 44th President of the United States, elected in 2008 and re-elected in 2012.
He was born in Honolulu in 1961, the son of Barack Obama Senior, a black Muslim and member of the Luo people from Kenya, and Stanley Ann Dunham, a white US-American from Kansas.
He finished studying political science at Columbia University, New York City in 1983 and studied a further three years at Harvard Law School, earning his PhD *magna cum laude*.
In 1996, he was elected senator in Illinois by the southern electoral district of Chicago, being renowned as a convinced left-liberal and social politician. His political breakthrough came with his keynote speech on the occasion of the Democratic Party Convention in 2004, followed by a landslide victory in the elections of January 2005, after which he became senator in the Capitol. On the national election day of 4 November in 2008, Obama and Joe Biden gained the necessary majority for their appointment as President and Vice-President, respectively, thus replacing the Republican Bush administration.
In 2009, Barack Obama was awarded the Nobel Peace Prize for his efforts to strengthen international diplomacy and the cooperation of peoples.

1. The title of this speech is "A New Beginning." Against the backdrop of what you have learned about US-Muslim relations, especially after 9/11, make an educated guess on a) why a new beginning might be necessary and b) the strategy employed by Obama in order to achieve his goal.

Listening

Netcode 40650-010

2. **Discuss** whether Obama conveys his message successfully; refer to your initial ideas on the strategies he might employ.

3. Do further research on reactions to Obama's speech in both the US as well as the Muslim world. Present your results in class and discuss to what extent speeches have the potential to bring about lasting change.

M3 America vs. The Narrative

Thomas L. Friedman

Thomas L. Friedman was prompted to write this article – an examination of Muslim-American relations eight years after 9/11 – after thirteen people were killed at Fort Hood in Texas. This comment was published in the *New York Times* on 29 November 2009.

Zoom in: People

Thomas L. Friedman

Thomas L. Friedman

Thomas L. Friedman is an internationally well-known author, reporter and columnist for the *New York Times*. He has won three Pulitzer Prizes so far and has written many best-selling books, including *From Beirut to Jerusalem* and *The World Is Flat*.

Friedman was born in Minneapolis, Minnesota in 1953 where he also attended university, graduating *summa cum laude* in 1975 with a degree in Mediterranean Studies. In 1978, he finished a degree in Modern Middle East Studies at Oxford University, afterwards working as a reporter for the London Bureau of United Press International, for example covering the civil war in Beirut where he lived from 1979 to 1981.

Joining the *New York Times* in May 1981, he was awarded the Pulitzer Prize for international reporting in 1983, especially for covering the events following the Israeli invasion of Lebanon. He received his second Pulitzer Prize for his work as the *Times*' Jerusalem Bureau Chief, during which time he also wrote his book *From Beirut to Jerusalem*.

From 1995 until today, Friedman has held the post of the *Times*' Foreign Affairs columnist. His columns are characterised by the belief that international relations are shaped by tensions between very old forces, such as nationalism and culture, and new ones, such as technology and the Internet.

In 2001, Friedman was awarded his third Pulitzer Prize for his examinations of the war in Afghanistan as well as terrorism and clashes between the Western and the Islamic world.

1. According to the MacMillan Dictionary, the noun "narrative" denotes "a story, or an account of something that has happened." What could this "narrative" possibly consist of in the context of Muslim-American relations?

2. **Point out** what "The Narrative" consists of, according to Friedman.

3. **Outline** what Friedman says about the American attitude towards the Muslim world on the one hand, and the Muslim world's attitude towards America on the other hand.

4. **Examine** the stance Friedman takes on this issue. Consider his line of argument and his choice of words.

What should we make of Maj. Nidal Malik Hasan, who apparently killed 13 innocent people at Fort Hood?*

Here's my take: Major Hasan may have been mentally unbalanced – I assume anyone who shoots up innocent people is. But the more you read about his support for Muslim suicide bombers, about how he showed up at a public-health seminar with a PowerPoint presentation titled "Why the War on Terror Is a War on Islam," and about his contacts with Anwar al-Awlaki, a Yemeni cleric* famous for using the Web to support jihadist violence against America – the more it seems that Major Hasan was just another angry jihadist spurred to action by "The Narrative."

What is scary is that even though he was born, raised and educated in America, The Narrative still got him.

The Narrative is the cocktail of half-truths, propaganda and outright lies about America that have taken hold in the Arab-Muslim world since 9/11.

Propagated by jihadist Web sites, mosque preachers, Arab intellectuals, satellite news stations and books – and tacitly* endorsed* by some Arab regimes – this narrative posits* that America has declared war on Islam, as part of a grand "American-Crusader-Zionist conspiracy" to keep Muslims down.

Yes, after two decades in which U.S. foreign policy has been largely dedicated to rescuing Muslims or trying to help free them from tyranny – in Bosnia, Darfur, Kuwait, Somalia, Lebanon, Kurdistan, post-earthquake Pakistan, post-tsunami Indonesia, Iraq and Afghanistan – a narrative that says America is dedicated to keeping Muslims down is thriving*.

Although most of the Muslims being killed today are being killed by jihadist suicide bombers in Pakistan, Iraq, Afghanistan and Indonesia, you'd never know it from listening to their world. The dominant narrative there is that 9/11 was a kind of fraud*: America's unprovoked onslaught on Islam is the real story, and the Muslims are the real victims – of U.S. perfidy*.

Have no doubt: we punched a fist into the Arab-Muslim world after 9/11, partly to send a message of deterrence*, but primarily to destroy two tyrannical regimes – the Taliban and the Baathists* – and to work with Afghans and Iraqis to build a different kind of politics. In the process we did some stupid and bad things. But for every Abu Ghraib, our soldiers and diplomats perpetrated a million acts of kindness aimed at giving Arabs and Muslims a better chance to succeed with modernity and to elect their own leaders.

The Narrative was concocted* by jihadists to obscure* that. […]

This narrative suits Arab governments. It allows them to deflect* onto America all of their people's grievances over why their countries are falling behind. And it suits Al Qaeda, which doesn't need much organization anymore – just push out The Narrative over the Web and satellite TV, let it heat up humiliated, frustated or socially alienated Muslim males, and one or two will open fire on their own. See: Major Hasan. […]

What to do? Many Arab Muslims know that what ails* their societies is more than the West, and that The Narrative is just an escape from looking honestly at themselves. But none of their leaders dare or care to open that discussion. In his Cairo speech last June, President Obama effectively built a connection with the Muslim mainstream. Maybe he could spark the debate by asking that same audience this question:

"Whenever something like Fort Hood happens you say, 'This is not Islam.' I believe that. But you keep telling us what Islam isn't. You need to tell us what it is and show us how its positive interpretations are being promoted in your schools and mosques. If this is not Islam, then why is it that a million Muslims will pour into the streets to protest Danish cartoons of the Prophet Muhammad, but not one will take to the streets to protest Muslim suicide bombers who blow up other Muslims, real people, created in the image of God? You need to explain that to us – and to yourselves."

Thomas L. Friedman, "America vs. The Narrative", www.nytimes.com, 28.11.2009 [06.09.2012]

Fort Hood is a military post located in Texas

cleric a leader of any religion

tacit expressed without being said directly
to endorse to express support, especially in public
to posit to say that sth. is true or should be accepted as true
to thrive to become very successful

fraud sth. that is not what people claim it is and designed to trick people
perfidy behaviour that shows that sb. cannot be trusted
deterrence *Abschreckung*
Ba'athism an ideology mixing Arab nationalism, pan-Arabism as well as Arab socialist and anti-imperialist interests, founded in Syria
to concoct to invent a false information or explanation, especially for dishonest purposes
to obscure to cover sth. so that it cannot be seen
to deflect to succeed in preventing sth. from being directed towards you
to ail to have a bad or harmful effect

5. At the end of his article, Friedman refers to Obama's Cairo Speech (cf. **M2**) and suggests a different question Obama should ask his audience. Taking into account your results from **M2** and **M3**, stage a debate between Obama and Friedman on the issue of Muslim-American relations.

M4 9/11 in History: Chapter or Footnote?

Dominic Streatfeild

Dominic Streatfeild is an author, journalist and producer who specializes in military and security issues. Among other things, he produced the Discovery Channel series *Age of Terror*, which examines the roots of political violence. The following text is an excerpt from his book *A History of the World Since 9/11: Disaster, Deception, and Destruction in the War on Terror.*

1. Against the backdrop of what you have learned about the 9/11 attacks so far, how would you answer the question raised in the title of this chapter?
2. **Give a summary** of Streatfeild's elaborations.
3. **Illustrate** Streatfeild's equation "uncertainty, certainty, opportunity" (l. 25) with the help of the text.
4. **Examine** how, or if, Streatfeild himself answers the question raised in the title of the chapter.
5. **Contrast** Streatfeild's analysis of Muslim-American relations with that of Friedman (cf. **M3**).

Historians like to break up human progress into bite-sized pieces. It's a useful technique: segregated and labelled, historical eras offer prisms through which to view the past, making it easier to comprehend. [...]

The impact of American Airlines Flight 11 into the North Tower of the World Trade Center at 8.46 a.m. on 11 September 2001 was immediately labelled a watershed event*. Seventy-six minutes later, after both the South Tower and the Pentagon had been hit, United Airlines Flight 93's calamitous* descent into a field in Shanksville, Pennsylvania, marked the end of the attacks – and the start of a still-ongoing attempt to define what, exactly, they mean. [...]

For politicians, as for historians, predictively labelling eras is a hazardous* procedure: history is littered with declarations of new eras that have somehow failed to materialize. In the aftermath of the attacks it seemed unreasonable to assume that 11 September would trigger a new way of thinking.

Did it?

In a hundred years, when schoolchildren discover what happened at the start of the twenty-first century, what will they think? Will they see the photographs of the collapsing towers, turn the page and forget them? Or will they learn that history stopped, then restarted in some new, fundamentally different direction? Will 9/11 be a chapter or a footnote?

Understandably, the first post-9/11 reaction was shock. [...] Within days, however, this sense of insecurity was overwhelmed by a counter-wave of certainty. America had been attacked because it was free. The perpetrators* were cowards. They were evil. We would

watershed event an event that causes an important change to take place
calamitous causing serious damage, or causing a lot of people to suffer
hazardous dangerous or harmful

perpetrator sb. who does sth. harmful, illegal, or dishonest get them. [...] The slate had been wiped clean*; now was the time to make a few changes. Now was the time to implement the policies we had always wanted, but never had the chance. In this sense, what 9/11 really offered policymakers was an opportunity. [...] This equation* – uncertainty, certainty, opportunity – paved the way for everything that happened next. Administration spokesmen announced that the United States was working on the dark side; that the gloves were coming off. Now was not the time to err* on the side of caution. If the goal was the greater good and the dissemination* of freedom, how could that be wrong? In the light of 9/11 and the need to protect its citizens from the "existential threat" of Osama bin Laden, the United States could have made a rational-sounding case for almost any policy decision.

It did.

In short order, America and her allies invaded Afghanistan, then moved on to Iraq. In the process, international alliances – NATO, the United Nations – were sidelined. Inside the country, civil liberties were curtailed*. US citizens were incarcerated* without trial or access to lawyers. Telephone lines and Internet hubs* were tapped. Dissent was quashed. Outside it, suspects were kidnapped, "rendered", then tortured and – in some cases – murdered. [...]

There's a school of thought that views terrorism as a provocation. Violence is involved, of course; civilians die. According to this theory, though, the actual deaths themselves are incidental*. The true aim of the terrorist atrocity* is not the carnage* it creates. The real objective is to push the target into a reaction – preferably an overreaction – that might conceivably further the protagonists' goals. [...] Seen in this light, 9/11 was not simply an atrocity but a political act with a political goal. Al Qaeda's aim in striking America was not to kill a few thousand workers but a more insidious* prodding*: Bin Laden wanted to provoke the United States. He was out to wake a sleeping giant. Results were immediately gratifying*.

Initially, war was declared on the terrorists responsible. Shortly afterwards, it was expanded to include terrorists everywhere, even those who had not been involved. Finally, war was launched against anybody who might become – at some point in the future – a terrorist. [...]

The moment the War on Terror was launched, all aspects of the new conflict were destined to spread. Those behind it saw it as a good thing: how could a war fought for democracy and freedom be anything other? Not everyone agreed. To many, the Global War on Terror was an aggressive campaign to export American power and, with it, the kind of hypocrisy* that had prompted the attacks in the first place. It was likely to prove counterproductive. Worse, the campaign would have far-reaching reverberations*. In all likelihood, these reverberations would outlast not only the war itself but also the administration that had launched it.

Were they right?

Dominic Streatfeild, "9/11 in History: Chapter or Footnote?", in: *A History of the World Since 9/11: Disaster, Deception, and Destruction in the War on Terror*, Atlantic Books, London 2011

a clean slate a situation in which everything bad or wrong you have done in the past is forgiven or forgotten and you can make a new start
equation *Gleichung*
to err to make a mistake
dissemination to make sth. available to a lot of people

to curtail to restrict
to incarcerate to put sb. in prison
hub the most important place where an activity takes place

incidental happening accidentally
atrocity a cruel and violent act
carnage a situation in which there is a lot of death and destruction
insidious dangerous or harmful
prodding motivation
gratifying making you feel pleased and satisfied

hypocrisy [hɪˈpɒkrəsi] *Heuchlerei*
reverberation an effect that spreads over a wide area or lasts for a long time

SPEAKING TEST

A speaking test as a substitute for a written exam will usually consist of two parts and you will probably take the test in pairs or in groups of three.

Part I

In Part I you must show that you can speak about a text or a visual for about ten minutes. You will be given a preparation time of thirty minutes to work on three tasks. These tasks cover the same skills as in a written test, so there will be a comprehension task, an analysis task as well as an evaluation task.

TIPS	
Make notes only. You are required to speak freely and to establish eye contact with the interlocutors.	✓
Watch your time management. You must deal with all three tasks sufficiently in ten minutes' time.	✓
Pay attention to the task instructions. Make sure you cover all aspects of the tasks	✓
The same rules apply as in a written test. So use your own words and neutral language in task one, apply the TEE-technique in task two and give a balanced assessment with reference to the text in task three.	✓
Your register must be formal.	✓
Guide your listeners through your talk. State what you are about to do and sum up your main results at the end of each task. Make use of varied sentence connectives.	✓
Speak slowly and clearly.	✓

M 5a On the Death of Osama bin Laden

Barack Obama

On 2 May 2011, Osama bin Laden was killed in Pakistan by a United States special forces unit, the Navy SEALs, in a CIA (Central Intelligence Agency) operation. The operation had been ordered by US President Barack Obama and was launched from Afghanistan. Within 24 hours of his confirmed death, the corpse of Osama bin Laden was buried at sea.
Though the UN, the EU, NATO and other governments approved of the killing, there were also dissenting voices, such as Amnesty International, who especially criticized the killing of an unarmed man instead of taking him into captivity. In the USA, especially in New York, public opinion was not just generally favourable towards the killing: people also celebrated it in many public places.
The given text is an extract from US President Obama's TV address to the nation, delivered on the day of bin Laden's death.

1. Outline Obama's message to the nation.
2. **Analyse** the rhetorical devices employed by the speaker to get his message across.
3. **Assess** whether the killing of Osama bin Laden can make up for the 9/11 traumata.

Netcode 40650-011

Good evening. Tonight, I can report to the American people and to the world that the United States has conducted an operation that killed Osama bin Laden, the leader of al Qaeda, and a terrorist who's responsible for the murder of thousands of innocent men, women, and children.
It was nearly 10 years ago that a bright September day was darkened by the worst attack on the American people in our history. [...] We quickly learned that the 9/11 attacks were carried out by al Qaeda – an organization headed by Osama bin Laden, which had openly declared war on the United States and was committed to killing innocents in our country and around the globe. And so we went to war against al Qaeda to protect our citizens, our friends, and our allies. [...] And so shortly after taking office, I directed Leon Panetta, the director of the CIA, to make the killing or capture of bin Laden the top priority of our war against al Qaeda, even as we continued our broader efforts to disrupt, dismantle*, and defeat his network. [...] Today, at my direction, [...] [a] small team of Americans carried out the operation with extraordinary courage and capability. No Americans were harmed. They took care to avoid civilian casualties*. After a firefight, they killed Osama bin Laden and took custody of his body.
For over two decades, bin Laden has been al Qaeda's leader and symbol, and has continued to plot attacks against our country and our friends and allies. The death of bin Laden marks the most significant achievement to date in our nation's effort to defeat al Qaeda. [...] The cause of securing our country is not complete. But tonight, we are once again reminded that America can do whatever we set our mind to. That is the story of our history, whether it's the pursuit of prosperity* for our people, or the struggle for equality for all our citizens; our commitment to stand up for our values abroad, and our sacrifices* to make the world a safer place. [...]

Barack Obama, "Osama Bin Laden Dead", www.whitehouse.gov, 02.05.2011 [06.09.2012]

to dismantle *here:* to end

casualty sb. who is injured or killed in an accident or a military action

prosperity wealth

sacrifice *Opfer*

Part II

Part II will usually be a collaborative task which you will work on with your partner(s) on a topic that requires you to keep up a conversation. You should also be prepared to answer questions asked by the interlocutor. Thus, the focus here is on communicative competences and participating in discussions. Part II is of roughly the same length as Part I.

TIPS	
Do not speak for too long, but give your partner a chance to contribute to the discussion.	✓
Make sure the discussion does not get stuck. You could, for example, ask for your partner's ideas or whether he/she agrees with you or not.	✓
When your partner is speaking, show that you are listening by reacting and responding appropriately. You could, for example, nod or smile as well as speak. If there is something you do not understand, ask for clarification.	✓
Watch your time management. You must deal with both tasks and you must also reach a conclusion. There will be further questions the interlocutor wants to ask you, too.	✓
Make use of varied phrases for expressing your opinion instead of a repetitive "I think". Otherwise the same language rules apply as in Part I.	✓

M 5b The American Public's Reactions to Osama bin Laden's Death

1. Provided below, there are various pictures which depict the American reaction to the death of Osama bin Laden. Together with your partner, describe the pictures. Take turns.

2. Decide which two pictures depict the most and the least appropriate reaction. Give reasons for your choice.

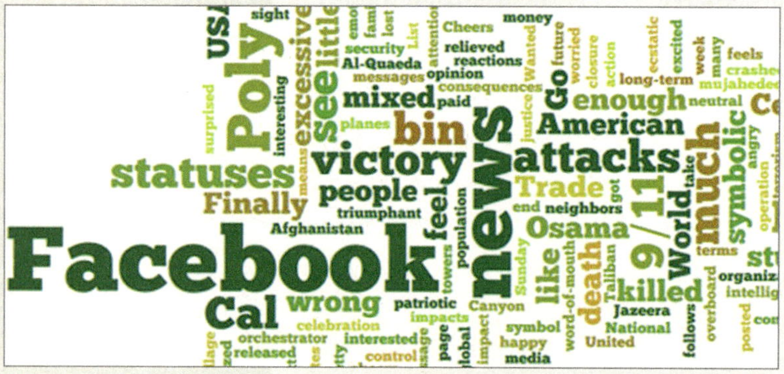

ZOOM IN: Words in Context

Preliminary Events: Paving the Way to 9/11?	
to be vexed at sth./sb.	über etw./jdn. verärgert sein
to equip sb. with sth.; equipment	jdn. mit etw. ausrüsten; Ausrüstung
to finance/fund sth./sb.	etw./jdn. finanzieren
to vilify; vilification	verteufeln/verunglimpfen; Verunglimpfung
extremist (n., adj.); extremism	Extremist/extremistisch; Extremismus
fanatic (n., adj.); fanatism	Fanatiker/fanatisch; Fanatismus
fundamentalist (n., adj.); fundamentalism	Fundamentalist/fundamentalistisch; Fundamentalismus
proxy war	Stellvertreterkrieg
terrorist (n., adj.); terrorism	Terrorist/terroristisch; Terrorismus
zealot	Fanatiker/Eiferer

The Sky Is Falling – The 9/11 Attacks	
to be bereaved; the bereaved	einen Verlust erlitten haben; die Hinterbliebenen/ Trauernden
to collapse (v., n.)	zusammenstürzen; Zusammensturz
to conspire against sth./sb.; conspiracy	sich gegen etw./jdn. verschwören; Verschwörung
to hijack (a plane); hijacker	(ein Flugzeug) entführen; Entführer
to premeditate sth.	etw. vorsätzlich planen
to suffer/experience a trauma; a traumatic experience	ein Trauma erleiden/erleben; ein traumatisches Erlebnis
anguish (of mind)	(Seelen-) Qual
atrocious (adj.); atrocity (n.)	grauenhaft/scheußlich; Gräueltat/Schreckenstat
bloodletting/bloodshed	das Blutvergießen
debris	Trümmer/Schuttmassen
rubble	Schutt
disarray	Unordnung/Verwirrung
disastrous; disaster	desaströs; Desaster
mayhem	Chaos

The Aftermath of 9/11: "Hunting Down Those Who Did It?"	
to accuse sb. of doing sth.; accusation	jdn. einer Sache beschuldigen; Anschuldigung
to annihilate; annihilation	etw. auslöschen; Auslöschung
to avenge sth./take revenge for sth.; avenger; revenge	für etw. Rache nehmen; Rächer; Rache
to blindside sb.	jdn. überrumpeln
to capture sb.; capture; captive	jdn. ergreifen; Gefangennahme; der Gefangene
to demolish; demolition	abreißen/zerstören; Zerstörung
to devastate; devastation	vernichten; Vernichtung
to expunge	auslöschen/vernichten
to harbour suspicions; suspicious (adj.); suspect (n.)	einen Verdacht hegen; verdächtig; der Verdächtige

The Aftermath of 9/11: "Hunting Down Those Who Did It?"	
to intervene; intervention	einschreiten/intervieren; Intervention
to level allegations against sb.	Vorwürfe gegen jdn. erheben
to liberate; liberation; liberator	befreien; Befreiung; der Befreier
to overthrow (v.; n.)	umstürzen; Umsturz
to pacify	befrieden
to retaliate; retaliation; retaliatory attack	etw. vergelten/sich rächen; Vergeltung; Vergeltungsschlag
to surrender (v., n.)	sich ergeben; Ergebung/Kapitulation
to wage (a) war against sb.	Krieg gegen jdn. führen
act of reprisal	Vergeltungsschlag
aftermath	Auswirkungen/Folgen
ambush	(Angriff aus dem) Hinterhalt
belligerent; belligerence	angriffslustig; Kriegslust
campaign	Feldzug/Kampf
casualty	(Todes-) Opfer
counter-attack	Gegenangriff
culprit	(Übel-) Täter, Angeklagter
germ warfare	biologische Kriegsführung
hostile; hostility	feindlich/feindselig; Feindseligkeit
missile	Geschoss, Rakete
patriotic; patriot; patriotism	patriotisch; Patriot; Patriotismus
pre-emptive war	Präventivschlag
reconnaissance	Erkundung/Auskundschaftung
retribution; retributive justice	Vergeltung; ausgleichende Gerechtigkeit
WMDs (Weapons of Mass Destruction)	Massenvernichtungswaffen

The Legacy of 9/11: Chapter or Footnote?	
to better/improve ≠ worsen/deteriorate international relations	internationale Beziehungen verbessern ≠ verschlechtern
to have a (beneficial ≠ disastrous) effect on sth.	(positive/vorteilhafte ≠ desaströse/katastrophale) Auswirkungen auf etw. haben
to leave a mark	Spuren hinterlassen
to recover; recovery	sich erholen; Erholung
far-reaching (consequences)	weitreichend(e) (Konsequenzen)
legacy	Hinterlassenschaft/Vermächtnis
long-term/short-term impact (on)	langfristige/kurzfristige Wirkung (auf)

ZOOM IN: Task Instructions (*Operatoren*)

Every exam you take in English consists of three tasks referring to three different performance standards (*Anforderungsbereiche, AFB*).

AFB I: Comprehension

Aspects to be considered:

- introduce your text by giving the essential information about the text at hand (author, title, text type, topic, publication, place, year, intention/target audience)
- use objective and neutral language
- use present tense and avoid contracted forms
- paraphrase (use your own words and do not use specific vocabulary which is also used in the text)
- make sure that your text is not longer than the original one
- do not state your own opinion
- do not quote

Task instruction	Definition
describe	Give a detailed account of something.
outline	Give the main features, structure or general principles of a topic, omitting minor details.
state	Specify clearly.
present	(Re-)structure and write down.
point out	Find and explain certain aspects.
summarize, write a summary	Give a concise account of the main points.

AFB II: Analysis

Aspects to be considered:

- use objective and neutral language
- use present tense and avoid contracted forms
- focus only on specific parts of the text
- stick to the appropriate terminology for analysing texts (cf. skills)
- look at the structure of the text and the stylistic devices and explain the resulting function/effect (one very effective method for doing this is the TEE-method)

T(hesis)	E(xample)	E(xplanation)
The author makes frequent use of alliterations/ enumerations/metaphors/ anaphoras/...	quote from the text	His/Her intention is to emphasize/stress/underline ...
In addition, he/she underlines his/her point by applying numerous contrasts ...	quote from the text	These contrasts make clear that ...

Task instruction	Definition
analyze, examine	Describe and explain in detail certain aspects and/or features of the text.
characterize	Describe and examine the way in which the character(s) is/are presented.
examine	cf. analyze
explain	Describe and define in detail.
illustrate	Use examples to explain or make clear.
interpret	Make clear the meaning of something.
compare	Point out similarities and differences.

AFB III: Evaluation

In the third task, you are either supposed to evaluate the text by giving your own opinion (Evaluation), or deal with the given information in a more creative way (Re-creation of text).

Aspects to be considered:

- use present tense and avoid contracted forms
- prove your points with reference to the text by quoting
- clearly state your personal opinion and give reasons for it
- explicity refer to what you have dealt with in class in regard to the topic

Task instruction	Definition
comment	Clearly state your opinion on the topic and support your views with evidence.
discuss	Investigate or examine by argument; give reasons for and against.
justify	Show adequate grounds for decisions or conclusions.
contrast	Emphasize the differences between two or more things.
assess	Find and explain certain aspects.

AFB III: Evaluation: Re-creation of text

The most common assignment for task three is to transfer the information from the given text into another text type. The text type will depend on whether the original text is a fictional or non-fictional text.

Aspects to be considered:

- use language appropriate for the respective text type (e. g. letter to the editor: formal, conversation/dialogue: (in)formal)
- make a connection to the given text
- be aware of the formal requirements

Task instruction	Definition
write ...	
– a newspaper article (report comment);	Appropriate language/register (report vs. comment) Differentiation concerning – facts, opinions – being objective, personalization/dramatization – particular case, context
– a speech script (talk, public/ formal speech, [debate] statement)	Appropriate language/register; Introduction: address of welcome/transparency of structure; Main part: structure and link to text/facts and assessment; Conclusion: e.g. summary/appeal
– a letter/e-mail (formal letter, letter to the editor; personal letter)	Appropriate language/register; author/addressee/reason for writing/form of address/complimentary close; structure: connection to topic, argumentation
– an interview	Appropriate language/register; neutral, unbiased, unemotional interviewer; Introduction (topic, conversational partner); Structured questioning; Conversational partners act according to their role
– an interior monologue/a conversation – an alternative ending (only advanced course)	Appropriate language/register; coherence between original and continued text

How to Analyse a Speech

Speeches are intended to persuade and win over an audience. Thus, it is impossible to find unbiased information or rhetoric, since facts and rhetorical devices have been carefully selected to serve the intention of the speech.

A good speech must have:

- **ethos:** positive qualities of the speaker, such as honesty, intelligence, or common sense, e. g.: "I was raised on the outskirts of LA, the son of a miner and a housewife."
- **pathos:** an appeal to the audience's emotions, e. g.: "Out of many, one. This has been the motto of the USA for centuries, and it always will be."
- **logos:** an appeal to the audience's reason, e. g.: "Every year, we spend 1.2 million dollars on military campaigns, but only 0.8 million dollars on education."

Factors which determine the level of formality, language as well as the complexity of the sentences:

(1) Circumstances of the speech	TV? Radio? Face-to-face?
(2) The speaker's position and role	Politician? Well-known public person?
(3) The audience	Mass audience (e.g. TV)? Limited audience? Friends or opponents?

1. Aspect of Analysis: Structure

In general, you should ask yourself how the speaker attempts to persuade the audience and to establish credibility while doing so. One aspect worth considering here is the **structure** of a speech.

A clear, argumentative structure makes it easy to follow the speaker's thoughts. It can also serve to manipulate the readership since we are usually inclined to believe something which appears to be logical at first glance. That is why the composition of a speech can help us to detect bias or manipulation attempts.

Means	Possible effect
Is there a clear statement or thesis in the introduction that is backed up in the following?	• immediate confrontation with the topic • to arouse expectations
Which connectives reveal the structure of the text?	• to indicate what is to follow • to emphasize and back up the thesis

Means	Possible effect
Is the structure antithetical, i.e. are opposing phenomena, positions/events/conclusions/words contrasted or compared directly?	• to illustrate developments • to show alternatives
Are the arguments illustrated with the help of examples?	• to simplify the matter • to appear credible and well-informed
How would you describe the degree of distance? Is there for example a change detectable from being very factual and distanced to being very involved and polemic?	• depending on the audience and the topic: to what degree is an emotional involvement of the audience considered to be necessary?
Is there a certain topic or motif that is recurrent?	• to make it easier to follow the line of argumentation • clear structure → memorable
Where is the emphasis in the conclusion? Is there a frame, i.e. does the speaker refer back to the introduction? Is there a call to action?	• to show the logical structure of the speech: thesis – proof in the main part – conclusion • call to action as a necessary consequence of the aforesaid facts

ZOOM IN: Vocabulary for Analysing the Structure of a Speech

The text divides neatly into ... parts/paragraphs.	*Der Text ist geschickt in ... Abschnitte unterteilt.*
The text consists of/compromises ... parts.	*Der Text besteht aus/umfasst ... Abschnitte.*
In the paragraph ... the speaker compares ... to ...	*Im ... Abschnitt vergleicht der Sprecher ... mit*
In the ... paragraph, the speaker passes from ... to ...	*Im ... Abschnitt geht der Sprecher von ... zu ... über.*
The paragraph forms a contrast to ...	*Der ... Abschnitt bildet einen Kontrast zu ...*
The whole speech is structured in an antithetical way.	*Die gesamte Rede ist antithetisch angelegt.*
The speaker puts forward/advances/uses/employs the argument that ...	*Der Sprecher führt das Argument an/benutzt das Argument, dass ...*
The speaker refutes/rebuts/disproves this argument by saying/claiming/arguing that ...	*Der Sprecher widerlegt/entkräftet dieses Argument, indem er sagt/behauptet/argumentiert, dass ...*
He/she illustrates/supports his/her argument by an example/a quotation/a comparison/a contrast.	*Er/sie veranschaulicht/unterstützt sein/ihr Argument mithilfe eines Beispiels/eines Zitats/eines Vergleichs/eines Kontrastes.*
The speaker (does not) go into details in regards to ...	*Der Sprecher geht (nicht) ins Details in Bezug auf ...*
He/she distinguishes/makes a distinction between ...	*Er/sie unterscheidet zwischen ...*
In the conclusion, the speaker summarizes/deduces/concludes that ...	*In der Schlussfolgerung fasst der Sprecher zusammen/leitet der Sprecher ab/schlussfolgert der Sprecher, dass ...*
His/her arguments are convincing/logical/inconsistent/manipulative.	*Seine/ihre Argumente sind überzeugend/logisch/widersprüch-lich/manipulativ.*

2. Aspect of Analysis: Rhetorical Devices

Rhetorical devices serve to convince the audience and are thus carefully selected by the speaker. Moreover, rhetorical devices can also manipulate the audience. Below is a list of some common devices and their possible effect.

Rhetorical device	Possible effect
repetition (v.: to repeat) • **anaphora:** a word or several words are repeated at the beginning of successive lines or sentences ("When we ... when we ... when we ...") • **alliteration:** the repetition of the same consonant sound in neighbouring words, usually at the beginning of words ("So soft, so sweet.") • **parallelism:** the repetition of similar or identical words, phrases or constructions in neighbouring lines, sentences, or paragraphs ("I like chocolate, I love chocolate.")	 • to emphasize key words words/major arguments/ important aspects • to increase the intensity
use of the **first-person plural pronoun** "we"	• to involve the listeners • to create the illusion of a group identity and a mutual understanding • to impose one's opinion on the listeners • to make it seem unreasonable not to agree with the speaker
rhetorical questions: to which the answer is obvious, or to which there is no clear answer	• to make the audience think or question old beliefs • to involve the audience • to arouse interest
enumeration (v.: to enumerate): the listing of words and phrases ("There were secretaries, craftspeople, office clerks, children in the tower.")	• to emphasize the extent of sth. • to make the listeners aware of the extent of a problem
imagery/figurative language • **simile:** an explicit comparison between two things which are basically quite different using "like" or "as" ("He was strong like a lion.") • **personification** (v.: to personify): representing animals, plants, inanimate objects or abstract ideas as if they were human beings and possessed human qualities ("The wind whispered her name.") • **metaphor:** a comparison between two things which are basically quite different without using "like" or "as"; while a simile says that one thing is LIKE another thing, a metaphor says that one thing IS another thing ("He is a lion.") • **symbol:** something concrete (like a person, object, image, word or event) stands for something abstract and invisible; the dove is a symbol of peace, for example	 • to arouse interest • to simplify complicated matters by referring to everyday or known experiences/phenomena
hyperbole/exaggeration/overstatement ("I am so hungry, I could eat a horse.")	• to launch into a polemic against sth./sb./to be polemic • to produce a humorous effect • to intensify an argument
direct address ("Would you want to spend all day working in a dirty office?")	• to make the listeners feel involved • to appeal to the listeners' conscience

Rhetorical device	Possible effect
antithesis/contrast: the contrasting of two opposing words, concepts, ideas	• to illustrate developments • to offer alternatives
climax: the arrangement of words, phrases, or clauses in an order of increasing importance, often in parallel structure ≠ **anti-climax:** the arrangement in an order of decreasing importance	• to draw attention to, for example, developments • to emphasize the impact of sth.
irony: saying the opposite of what you really mean **sarcasm:** a strong form of verbal irony used to hurt sb. through mockery or disapproval	• to utter indirect criticism • to appear witty • to establish a connection with the audience, presupposing they share the speaker's critical view
prolepsis/procatalepsis: refuting anticipated objection ("Some people might say that ... but this is not true because ...")	• to appear well-informed • to establish credibility

ZOOM IN: Vocabulary for Analysing Rhetorical Devices

In order to convince/manipulate the audience, the speaker makes use of/employs several rhetorical devices.	Der Sprecher verwendet mehrere rhetorische Mittel, um sein Publikum zu überzeugen/manipulieren.
By employing/using ..., the speaker stresses/underlines/ emphasizes/puts emphasis on ...	Indem der Sprecher ... benutzt/verwendet, betont er, dass ...
The (metaphor) in line ... suggests/illustrates/expresses that ...	Die (Metapher) in Zeile ... suggeriert/veranschaulicht/ drückt aus, dass ...
The (personification) of ... hints at/makes clear/shows that ...	Die (Personifizierung) von ... deutet an/verdeutlicht/zeigt, dass ...
... is personified in order to ...	... wird personifiziert, um zu ...

3. Aspect of Analysis: Style, Tone, Register

As mentioned above, the circumstances of the given speech as well as the speaker's position and the addressed audience determine the style of the speech.
Style is a term for the way of speaking, so it can refer to the choice of words, the tone, grammar and techniques. **Tone** describes the general feeling or attitude towards the subject of the speech which creates a certain mood. The **register** a speaker uses is closely related to style. The register can be formal or informal and often reflects the social status of the people.

Features of formal style:	formal expressions, foreign words, specialist terms, objectivity, detachment, politeness, complete and complex sentences
Features of informal style:	informal and colloquial expressions, phrasal verbs, simple sentences, subjectivity, can contain slang or even rude and vulgar expressions, incomplete or grammatically incorrect sentences

By means of style, tone and register, speakers can exert a lot of influence on their audience, especially if they intend to create a certain group identity and to establish an emotional connection to their listeners, for example by showing that they are on the same level as the audience and understand what is important to them.

Zoom in: Vocabulary for Analysing Style, Tone, Register

The speaker uses everyday/colloquial/informal/vulgar expressions.	Der Sprecher verwendet alltägliche/umgangssprachliche/informelle/vulgäre Ausdrücke.
specialist terms	Fachbegriffe
The style of the speech is elevated/sophisticated/academic/concise/objective/impersonal/formal/informal/intimate.	Der Stil der Rede ist gewandt/geistreich/gehoben/raffiniert/akademisch/prägnant/objektiv/unpersönlich/formal/informell/vertraulich.
The tone of the speech is humorous/ironic/serious/critical/friendly/positive/light-hearted/neutral.	Der Ton der Rede ist humorvoll/ironisch/ernst/kritisch/freundlich/positiv/unbeschwert/neutral.
The moderate/angry is tone is intended to ...	Der gemäßigte/wütende Ton bezweckt ...
The passage is full of/abundant with taboo terms/Latin expressions/loan words.	Der Abschnitt enthält sehr viele Tabu-Begriffe/lateinische Ausdrücke/Lehnwörter.
vivid/animated/exaggerated language	anschauliche/lebendige/übertriebene Sprache
The speaker has a polite/impolite/rude/blunt way of addressing the issue/the audience.	Der Sprecher hat eine höfliche/unhöfliche/unverschämte/unverblümte Art, Probleme/das Publikum anzusprechen.
The speaker applies this word in a figurative/neutral/wide/pejorative sense.	Der Sprecher verwendet dieses Wort in einem übertragenen/neutralen/breiten/pejorativen Sinn.
The phrase/expression means/denotes/implies/stands for ...	Die Phrase/der Ausdruck bedeutet/kennzeichnet/impliziert/steht für ...
He/she mainly uses words from the semantic field of ...	Er/sie benutzt vorwiegend Wörter des Wortfeldes ...
The word ... suggests that/evokes associations with ...	Das Wort ... suggeriert, dass/erweckt Assoziationen mit ...
He/she predominantly employs words that are connoted positively/negatively.	Er/sie benutzt vorwiegend positiv/negativ konnotierte Wörter.